Along the River
that Flows Uphill

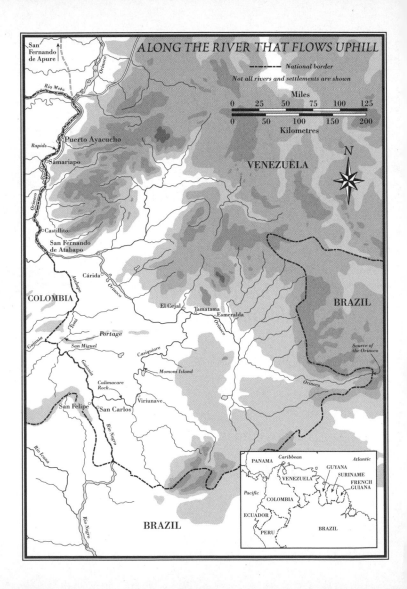

Along the River that Flows Uphill

From the Orinoco to the Amazon

by
Richard Starks and
Miriam Murcutt

HAUS PUBLISHING
London

 ArmchairTraveller

First published in Great Britain in 2009 by Haus Publishing Ltd,
70 Cadogan Place, London SW1X 9AH
www.hauspublishing.co.uk

Copyright © 2009 Richard Starks and Miriam Murcutt

The moral rights of the authors have been asserted.

A CIP catalogue record for this book is available from the
British Library

ISBN 978-1-906598-32-7

Typeset in Garamond by MacGuru Ltd
Printed and bound in the UK by J F Print
Jacket illustration: Getty Images

Contents

1

An Intrepid and Fearless Explorer

I've nearly died three times in my life – which is funny in an ironic way, since I was once accused of never taking any risks.

The first time was in northern Canada where I nearly died of exposure: the car I was driving hit a passing moose, spun into a ditch, and in the middle of winter left me eighty-five snow-filled miles from the nearest outpost of what locally passed for civilization. The second time was in the Himalayas where I nearly died of boredom: a ferocious blizzard trapped me in a hut for eight interminable days and nights. The third time was in Venezuela where a Yanomami Indian threatened to shoot me with a poisoned arrow.

Or maybe it was in Colombia where FARC guerillas tried to take me hostage.

Either way, the third time was on a trip I took up the Orinoco to see a strange river called the Casiquiare.

～

The chances are you've never heard of the Casiquiare. Most people haven't, even though, like the source of the Nile or the exact location of Timbuktu, it once created so much controversy that the mere mention of its name could spark a physical fight among geographers in Europe. That was back in the 18th century when large parts of the world were still blank spaces – ones that map-makers filled with billowing images of a pucker-lipped Wind, or the beguiling words set in Olde English type, '𝕳𝖊𝖗𝖊 𝕭𝖊 𝕯𝖗𝖆𝖌𝖔𝖓𝖘'.

Travellers who claimed they had peered into those empty spaces came back with tall tales of two-headed monsters, Amazon women, and fire-breathing giants with backward-facing feet. They also came back with tall tales of the Casiquiare – a river so fantastic that it could do the impossible and flow uphill.

⟿

These days, the Casiquiare is all but forgotten, and I might have forgotten it too, had I not, as a child, longed to be an old-time explorer. I yearned to go where no other man had set foot – to be first to penetrate lands so remote that not even meridians dared to cross them. I could not do that, of course. Not as a child, and not in a world that was mapped to the inch. So instead I read books – hundreds of books – about my explorer-heroes and the adventures they'd faced, and in one of these books – about an expedition through the stifling heat of the Amazon jungle – I stumbled upon this extraordinary river.

The Casiquiare is unique. There is, quite literally, no other river like it on the face of the planet. Somehow, it manages to unite two river systems that should, by rights, be entirely separate. The two river systems are the Orinoco and the Amazon, and by joining them together, the Casiquiare performs the astonishing feat of flowing *up and over* the watershed that divides them. I did not understand how it could do that.

⌐

I never expected to see this remarkable river, but in the spring of 2005, I fired off a string of emails to a select group of magazine editors to suggest story ideas for travel articles I wanted to write. I had been doing this – with my writing partner, Miriam Murcutt – for several years, and nearly every editor we approached had studiously ignored our proposals. But then – out of the blue – one of the editors said "Yes". He liked the idea of an article about the Casiquiare, and, better still, was willing to offer a small advance to secure it.

I was so inured to rejection that I'd long abandoned any idea that I might actually be asked to follow through and make one of the journeys I'd been proposing. The journeys were daydreams. Castles in the air.

But now, here I am with Miriam, trapped on a boat one thousand miles up the Orinoco as we fight our way towards the Casiquiare. The rain has eased, but the humidity still wraps itself around me like a blanket, curling the pages of my notebook and blurring the words even as I write them. I am sweating profusely. I am covered in bites. And secretly I'm wondering if I haven't made an appalling mistake and exposed myself to too much risk.

〜

Beyond the travel books I've read, little in my life has prepared me for the ordeal that is the Casiquiare. I was born in England, and grew up there, and in the United States and Scotland, where, for reasons I now find hard to explain, I studied theoretical chemistry at the University of Aberdeen. I emigrated to Canada and found work as a financial journalist, writing about personal investment and white-collar crime. I wrote a few books, including the novelization of a horror movie-script by the director David Cronenberg (which I wrote in the mornings); and a slim economics text book on the declining role of manufacturing (which I wrote in the afternoons).

My "one year" in Canada turned into ten, and when I returned to England, I found myself out of place as well as out of work, until, with Miriam, I launched a small publishing business that proved surprisingly lucrative as well as resilient. When we later sold up, we moved to Colorado – to be close to the mountains – and nurtured optimistic plans to develop what, for me, has since turned into a stop-go, on-off career as a writer. I'm sure, from the outside, that I appear to lead an ordered life, but deep down I'm every bit as confused as my past. I would like to go home again, but although I have acquired three nationalities – British, Canadian and American – or perhaps *because* I have acquired three nationalities, I no longer know where that home is. So when I'm not writing, I keep on the move, and travel.

∽

The article I've been commissioned to write is for *Geographical*, the official magazine of the Royal Geographical Society of London. I find this exhilarating.

For someone like me with a childhood ambition to be an explorer, there can be no higher master to serve.

The Royal Geographical Society – or simply the "Society", as it is known – was founded in 1830, soon after Britain and France, the two great explorer nations of the 17th and 18th centuries, ceased to fund expeditions that for the most part were run by their navies. Exploration became the preserve of the individual, belonging to courageous, resourceful men. Men of character and resolve. Men who were giants – like Livingstone, Burton, Speke, Grant and Baker. Men who were my heroes, and with whom, in my imagination at least, I felt I should be standing.

It was Livingstone – sent by the Society – who tried to settle the burning issue of the source of the Nile and so put an end to the bitter dispute that raged between Burton and Speke, both of whom claimed to have solved that particular mystery. In the eyes of Sir Roderick Murchison, one of the Society's founders and several times its president, Livingstone stood head and shoulders above even the other giants. He was, in Murchison's words, "as noble and lion-hearted an explorer as ever lived," so inevitably, Livingstone was the man I admired most. But the man with whom I *identified* most was the one who travelled to Africa to find him – the one who famously, and no doubt apocryphally, uttered the immortal words that were once seared into the heart of every English schoolboy, "Dr. Livingstone, I presume." That man, of course, was Henry Morton Stanley.

Stanley appeals to me because he possessed a seriously flawed character. He, too, worked as a journalist and writer. He felt ambivalent about his nationality – he was British by birth and American by choice. And he was driven by an insatiable desire to prove himself. He also suffered from recurring bouts of doubt and depression, which he avoided by living all his life in a flurry of motion. If he succeeded at all – and he undoubtedly did – then he did so in spite of, rather than because of, himself. Stanley was a man I might not have liked, but he was one I feel sure I would have understood.

The Society that so admired Livingstone (and initially rejected Stanley) was once located on London's Savile Row, but now it operates from a sprawling complex on Kensington Gore. I went there, many years ago, to hear Sir John Hunt describe the 1953 expedition that he led to the summit of Everest. The building reeked of Victoriana. Its Russian-pine floorboards creaked, its wood-paneled walls looked sombre, and the paintings that hung on them – of long-dead presidents and Gold Medal winners – were dark, baleful and intended to impress. Sir John himself personified that long-gone era. Trim, dapper, with a full head of white hair, he spoke in a clipped, understated style that I'm sure fearless explorers have always employed. As they strode across plains or hacked their way through jungles, these explorers would affect a sweeping contempt for any setback or danger. Insurmountable obstacles became "a bit of a holdup", while spear-throwing tribes of screaming natives were routinely dismissed as "not awfully keen to see us."

At the heart of the Society, at least for me, stands its magnificent library, with more than 150,000 books on every aspect of geography and travel. There's a map room, too, with nearly one million maps, charts, atlases and expedition reports, as well as a picture gallery that holds a unique collection of sketches and paintings – including more than forty by Thomas Baines, the Society artist who travelled with Livingstone on his 1858 expedition to the Zambesi.

The library holds many of the titles I read as a child – most notably *Through the Dark Continent* and *How I Found Livingstone*, both written by Stanley. My own copies of these two classics sit on my shelves still – alongside Rider Haggard's *King Solomon's Mines*, Joseph Conrad's *Lord Jim*, and, of course, *Heart of Darkness* (with Marlow as Stanley and Kurtz as Livingstone). In books like these – old-fashioned tales of trial and adventure – the hero typically embarks on a long and treacherous journey, often up a river, and always in a life-or-death struggle to prove himself and discover what kind of person he really is.

It occurs to me, as I review my commission, that *Geographical* is offering me the same opportunity – the chance to make a long and difficult journey along a remote and dangerous river that, intriguingly, comes with a mystery attached. It's an opportunity not just to travel and write, but also to discover if, as an adult, I have what it takes to be what I wanted to be as a child – an intrepid and fearless *Boy's Own Annual* hero-explorer.

It seems ideal.

～

Miriam, of course, has no such motivation. But I dislike travelling alone, so when I pitch the idea of journeying the length of the Casiquiare, I take a devious approach.

The two of us have recently returned from a crossing we made of the Tibetan plateau. That journey – part of the research for another book we wrote – took place in the middle of winter, so it was high, dry and cold. This one will be low, wet and hot – a perfect antidote, I say. Miriam is not impressed. A week in Paris would be a better antidote. And anyway, we both enjoyed our Tibetan adventure. We don't need an antidote.

"There'll be insects," she says.

"Perhaps. Maybe one or two."

This is an obvious lie. There are a zillion insects in this world, and all the serious ones that bite, suck or sting live in the Orinoco and Amazon basins.

"Plus we'll be stuck on a boat," she says.

"But not for long," I tell her.

This, too, is a transparent lie. The journey I'm proposing will take us along nearly one thousand miles of river. So of course we'll be stuck on a boat.

I still don't know why she has agreed to join me. It could be that she's foolhardy enough to try anything. But also, I think, she secretly harbours a perverse desire to visit the Yanomami – a remote tribe of Indians I know we'll encounter – who, fairly or not, are reputed to be "the most violent people on Earth."

2

Where the Road Ends and the River Begins

We leave on Thursday, August 4th, on a late-afternoon flight to Caracas. As we board the plane, I am – as always when I fly – thinking about the Second Law of Thermodynamics. It's one of the hazards of a science-based education.

As I understand it, the Second Law says two things about the Universe we live in. One is that energy tends to *decrease* – which helps to explain why rivers (other, apparently, than the Casiquiare) flow downhill and not uphill. The other is that entropy tends to *in*crease – which helps to explain why time flows towards the future and not the past.

Entropy has a number of definitions, but to my mind it is best seen as a measure of disorder. It is everywhere around us, but, like Newton's gravity, it hides in plain sight, so obvious it is often overlooked. But if you drop a china teacup onto a tile floor, the cup will shatter, because a cup is more ordered than the pieces it breaks into, so by dropping the cup, you have raised the disorder. You have boosted the entropy. This process never works in reverse. You never drop the pieces and then look down to find they've reassembled into a cup – because if you did, then time would be flowing backwards, away from the future and towards the past. And time never seems to do that.

A plane, of course, is a more ordered structure than a china teacup. If you take it up to 30,000 feet and bring it safely down to Earth again, you may not have boosted its entropy – unless a part falls off, say, or merely manages to work itself loose – but one day, I can't help thinking, the plane will try to grab as much entropy as it can. It will come down, and, like a dropped teacup, be shattered into a large number of disordered pieces. I don't know if this is scientifically correct, since

I'm never sure where closed systems end and open ones begin. But entropy, to me, is a key component of the inherent chaos that pervades much of our lives.

⌒

It is nearly midnight by the time we clear customs at Simón Bolívar airport – not a good time to be here, since the airport is a notoriously dangerous place, especially after dark. "Caracas," I had read on the Internet, "is a city with a reputation for violence; it has a murder rate four times higher than that of Medellín, Colombia, so make sure you arrive during the day." Deplaning passengers are often attacked and robbed on the fifty-yard walk from the terminal to the taxi stand; or they are lured into unmarked cars, posing as taxis, and driven to a desolate spot and assaulted there.

Part of this problem stems from the bolívar – Venezuela's oil-based currency – which is not fully convertible, so is hard to buy outside the country. At the same time, credit cards and travellers' cheques have little application beyond Caracas; and ATMs, although quite numerous, have the annoying habit of taking your card but not dispensing your cash. Most visitors therefore arrive in the country with large wads of foreign bills secreted about them, which means they are much more likely to be met by money-changers and muggers than they are by family and friends. A common trick is for a money-changer to offer a seductively high rate, and then, when you succumb, to have a mugger-accomplice relieve you of your bolivars as soon as you exit the building.

Two things we have therefore determined: one, we will not change money at the airport, and two, we will not climb into any unmarked cars. To preclude these two possibilities, we have arranged for a driver to meet us, but, of course, the Universe is subject not just to the Second Law, but also to Murphy's Law, so when we arrive, our driver does not.

Half an hour after we land, we are hunched in a doorway exchanging dollars for bolivars, and half an hour after that, we are sitting in the back of a *pirata* – an unmarked "taxi" – riding through the night and the long, dark tunnels that lead into Caracas.

We bounce around on ripped seats, feeling metal springs dig into our backs. Black tape holds the dashboard together, and a crucifix jerks and jangles from a rubber sucker high on the windshield. I watch the driver's eyes in his rear-view mirror. I am more than a little wary, but his gaze seems friendly enough, and Miriam is able to draw him out by practising her new-found Spanish.

We emerge from the tunnels and reach the edge of the city. Litter rustles in the gutters so the pavements appear to shimmy and sway. The streets are dark, but high above us, *ranchos*, or slums, cling to the hills, their lights showing dimly like distant stars. The air hangs heavy with smog, and as we approach the centre, the potholes, if anything, seem to get deeper.

The driver talks about his family – his brothers and sisters, and his six children. Four boys, two girls.

"They are a blessing," he says, then hesitates a moment, inclining his head to one side. "Sometimes," he adds.

He reaches up to touch the crucifix on his windshield, but I can't tell if he's thanking the Catholic Church for the size of his family – or blaming it.

Caracas by day looks little better than Caracas by night. We ride the subway to Bellas Artes, and emerge into a brown haze that casts the city in a sepia light. The *museo* we want to visit is a concrete building cut off from the centre by a busy road and a patch of dead grass. As we circle the building, looking for a way in, we are hit by the smell of stale urine, which rises from the steps and the walkways. Barbed wire guards one entrance, broken glass another, and slowly it dawns on us that the museum is closed – and not, perhaps, just for the day.

We change course and cross Avenida México, heading towards Paradero and the Guaicaipuro market. Some of the buildings we pass have corrugated roofs and exterior wiring. Others look abandoned, with steel cores waving like feelers from the tops of their concrete supports. Over everything hangs a pall of smoke and the acrid smell of burning rubbish.

Caracas sits in a high bowl surrounded by mountains, and when it was young – in the 16th century – its elevation offered welcome relief from the heat and humidity of the coastal plain. The air in the bowl was pure and sweet, the skies a constant, cobalt blue. But now, fumes fill the bowl as the residents breathe the wastes of an extended oil boom that has made a few of them rich. In the *ranchos* on the hills, the poor look down as if from the bleachers. They are part of the city – in fact, because of their numbers, they *are* the city – but they are still excluded from the gated high-rises and guarded towers that mark the commercial core. Each day, they trek down the hillsides, driven in part by a desperate boredom, but also by the hope that, perhaps today, they might find an edge, an angle to work, an opportunity to exploit.

In the *mercado*, a group of them watch us walk by – Miriam in particular, who, because of her height and her fair hair, stands out as an obvious outsider. One of them calls out to us –

"*Eh! Americanos!*"

– and we make the mistake of turning to look. We've given ourselves away. You can be anything in Caracas, but not an American.

A wave of hostility washes towards us, like heat rising from the pavement, and more people start to shout.

"*Eh! Americanos! Eh! Putos!*"

They move towards us, closing in. We know better than to run, but we push through the crowd and head back to the subway. We've experienced anti-Americanism before, but nothing as overt as this. As long as George W. Bush is president – and condones torture and extraordinary rendition – it's hard to travel *anywhere* as an American. But here in Caracas, the hatred for *gringos* has been deliberately fuelled by Hugo Chávez, who, like Bush, needs an enemy to sustain him, and by Pat Robertson, a TV evangelist and one-time US presidential candidate, who recently called, in a kind of Christian *fatwa*, for Chávez to be murdered by the CIA.

Back at our hotel, we collect our passports. I have brought my American one with me, as it allows me to get in and out of the United States, but I am not travelling on it. Nor am I using my British passport, following Tony Blair's devoted support for Bush's invasion of Iraq. Instead, I rely on my Canadian one.

As I slip it into my pocket, I think back to the day I became a Canadian citizen and stood on a Toronto street, looking up at a skyline that was being transformed by yet another wave of high-rise development. Towering over the city was a crane, owned by one of the new construction companies that symbolized the opportunities that Canada presented to immigrants like me. A banner, the size of a field, hung from the crane, proudly displaying the name of the company. In the US, that name could have been Turner Construction. In the UK, it might have been Taylor Woodrow. But that day in Toronto, the name on the banner was

KOWALSKI and WONG

and I thought, yes, that's Canada.

∽

We leave Caracas the following morning, catching a bus south to Maracay – a polluted industrial sprawl that's absurdly nicknamed "the Garden City". Later, we pass through green, pleasant mountains before setting out to cross the vast plains of the *llanos*. This is Venezuela's prairie – cowboy country, with huge ranches, or *hatos*, that match any of the spreads in the Australian outback or the American west. It is also the site of a crude land-redistribution program that Chávez has been aggressively promoting.

In Venezuela, about 75 percent of the land rests in the hands of just 5 percent of the owners, an after-effect of the country's colonial era, which saw most of the wealth controlled by a handful of *caudillos* – strong men with military followings – who fought during Venezuela's war of independence from Spain. Much of this land lies fallow, in large estates called "*latifundios*", because the wealthy owners – sometimes corporations – cannot profitably farm it. Chávez wants *campesinos*, or peasants, to occupy the land and put it to work, hoping that this "redistribution" will boost the country's production of food. There are, however, growing fears that his makeshift initiative – like so many other government programs – will yield precisely the opposite effect and create a decline in output, as Mugabe found in Zimbabwe.

We need two days to cross the *llanos*. It's the rainy season, and the grasslands are flooded. The three major rivers we pass – the Apure, the Capanaparo and the Meta, all significant tributaries of the Orinoco – run bloated and swollen, sometimes overflowing their banks. Buffalo stand up to their bellies in water, and scores of birds sit like fruit in the trees. Herons, or *garzas*, abound – their white plumage as bright as snowdrops in a winter garden.

We spend the night in San Fernando de Apure, a cross-roads town with broken sidewalks and puddled streets. We stand out here as we did in Caracas, but people only track us with their eyes. The next day we push on. The road deteriorates, narrowing to a muddy track, but the driver's helper – a young boy in baggy shorts and a string vest – keeps piling up sacks and boxes as ever more passengers squeeze on board. Soon we're sitting in a mobile sauna, bumping along with fat, brown strangers squashed onto our laps.

Near San Juan de Payara, a man clambers on. He

wears a blue tee-shirt with a white slogan emblazoned across his chest.

Oooh, aaah
Chávez no va

His message is that Chávez doesn't "go" – meaning his presidency doesn't work – and it's a play on the pro-Chávez slogan,

Oooh, aaah
Chávez no se va

which means exactly the opposite, that Chávez *won't* be going, because his presidency *does* work. An argument starts, and insults get batted around like a ping-pong ball.

"Only a *tonto* – a moron – would vote for Chávez."

"Oh, yeah? You'd thank him if you ever got sick."

"I can't afford to get sick. Have you seen what he's done to prices? I have to keep running just to stand still."

"At least he's on the side of the *campesinos*."

"He's a politician. He's on his own side, just like the others."

The banter is good-natured, a way to pass the time. Miriam joins in, practising her Spanish and shamelessly switching sides to keep the argument going. But the man in the blue tee-shirt suddenly stands up, angrily shouting. The fun has been drained out of the discussion. The driver's helper steps in to cut it short, cranking up the bus' speakers to blast out a wall of sound with a bass so loud I can feel it vibrating my rib cage.

⌒

At Puerto Ayacucho – the river port that's our immediate destination – we are confronted by a convoy of jeeps packed with gun-toting soldiers. Battered cars block the roads, and the pavements are mobbed by people waving flags and shouting slogans.

It's election time in Venezuela, mainly affecting local-government officials – but here in Amazonas, the state governor is fighting for his political life, and tensions are running high. The National Guard is out on the streets, ready to stamp out any riots before they begin. The soldiers have a permanent base here in town, because Puerto Ayacucho is on the border with Colombia and serves as a transit stop for drugs – mainly cocaine – that are smuggled out of that country en route to Europe and the United States.

Because of the elections, the few hotels are all full, but we find a room above an auto-repair shop not far from the centre. It has bars on the window and double locks on the door. When the afternoon rains empty the street, I gaze out at corrugated iron roofs and stores that are heavily fortified with grilles. The rain tips down, drumming hard on the metal, and within minutes small rivers run down the street, washing away some of the rubbish. As the rain stops, we venture outside, ducking under the plastic sheets that have been strung up by shopkeepers who are selling goods from the pavement and want to keep their customers dry. The plastic sags under the weight of water, threatening to douse us, but it wouldn't matter much if it did. The rain may have stopped, but the air remains clogged with moisture. We are both dripping and limp with sweat.

We walk across town, past small shops that sell electrical goods, cheap shirts, ladies' underwear, flip-flops and jeans, then splash through what, in the dry season, might be a football pitch, but now is a lake with a goalpost at either end. On the far side of town, we find a large general store set back from the main road. Ladders lean against the wall outside, with tiers of buckets – half-full of water – stacked beneath them. Inside, we hunch under a low wooden ceiling and peer through the gloom. Piles of stock lie strewn around – picks, shovels, knives, cans, nails, rope, basins, saws, plastic sheeting, metal grilles, sacks of flour, and still more ladders and buckets.

We root around until we locate the rolled tobacco we've come for, spread out on newspaper-lined shelves in a corner at the back. The tobacco comes in long, twisted ropes, like dreadlocks, and seems lank and dank, every bit as musty as the store – but, we've been told, this is just what we need to help us curry favour when we later encounter the fearsome Yanomami. We also find the Number Ten fish-hooks the Yanomami supposedly like, hidden away in small, wooden drawers, neatly marked by size and weight. We buy several dozen of the hooks, along with a similar number of leaded weights.

"And you must take cloth," the shopkeeper tells us. He reels it out with spindly arms. "The Yanomami like cloth." His voice is as flat as his expression. "But it must be red, the colour of blood."

❧

The next day, we take a taxi around the Atures and Maipures rapids – a fifty-mile-long tumble of rocks and pour-offs that for centuries have sealed off the upper Orinoco from the outside world. It is here, at a settlement called Samariapo, that the road ends and river travel begins. On my map, Samariapo looks like a small town, but on the ground, it embraces a few tacky sheds and one or two huts selling snacks, sweets and soft drinks.

Under a gray sky, I walk down to the river for my

first proper look at the upper Orinoco. Standing here, I am nearly eight hundred miles from the sea, yet looking out across the river, I can see that it's two – even three – miles wide, a huge highway of water that slides through the jungle like a giant anaconda. I bend down and scoop some of its water into my hands. The river itself appears a murky brown, but the water I hold is almost clear. I turn my head and look upstream, at the dense walls of jungle – ripe with mystery and promise – that line each bank.

I look at my map. The Orinoco is clearly marked, like a crack in the Earth that could be seen from space. A few settlements dot its banks, but away from the river, in the vast areas where the jungle casts its mantle of green, there is nothing – not even a contour. At long last, I think, I have arrived at a place where it can still legitimately be said, "**Here be Dragons**".

3

"Relax: Things Can Only Get Worse"

As a child, I used to play a simple drawing game. One person would sketch a head on a piece of paper – a human head, perhaps, or maybe the head of an animal, or even that of an alien. He would then fold the paper over to hide the head, but leave a couple of lines showing to indicate where the neck ended, and pass the paper to the next player, who would draw a body – any kind of body – attaching it to the neck. The second player would fold the paper over to hide the body and give the drawing to a third person, who would add legs. And so it would go until the feet were added, the drawing was complete, and the paper could be unfolded – at which point, everyone would see, with great delight, what kind of aberrant creature they had created.

I'm reminded of this game when I catch sight of the boat that is going to be our home for the next one thousand miles. The boat – the *Iguana* – is moored about thirty yards offshore, and it looks to me as if it has been put together with spare parts plundered at random from other boats. It has no lines, no flow. Nothing runs the length of the boat except the hull and the waterline. Instead, at the bow, a wheelhouse sits like an outhouse on top of a couple of cabins; while near the stern, a flat structure like a shipping container balances precariously on the hull. These various shapes have been painted in arbitrary kindergarten colours – red, blue, white, yellow and black – so that the boat sits in the water like a toy in a baby's bathtub.

"It's a pantomime horse," Miriam says, "with a head that doesn't know what its tail is doing."

I look around. There are several people milling about – men, women and children – and among them we find our guide, Lucho, and his wife, Natalia, whom we meet now for the first time. Lucho is a part-white, part-Baré Indian, about forty years old, with a pot-scourer mass of abandoned black hair, and room for the wind to whistle through the notable gap between his front teeth. He's shorter than I am, but if he lacks anything in height he more than makes up for it in brawn. I know little of his past, but as the owner of the *Iguana*, he earns his living ferrying travellers along the upper Orinoco – and the Casiquiare, too – as far as Manaus in Brazil. He also serves as an introduction to the fierce Yanomami, since he once lived among them for more than a year, and so speaks their language and has a deep understanding of their lifestyle and culture.

Natalia is a few years younger and several shades lighter. A Puerto Rican – which helps explain her grasp of both English and Spanish – she has, until now, been our main point of contact. She runs the business side of Lucho's operation, and seeks up-front payment before we set off. She is polite, but insistent. She is also, we see, a recent mother with a squirming baby clinging on to her long strands of hair as it breast-feeds beneath her hitched-up tee-shirt.

I had not expected the baby, but looking across at the *Iguana*, I judge that there should be room enough on board for five.

Lucho is busy and clearly distracted as he checks permits and supplies. Several of the people milling about appear to be helping, stacking up goods and ferrying them out to the *Iguana*. One of them approaches – a swarthy young man, about twenty years old, with a nascent belly that swells over his trousers like a water-filled balloon. He greets me with a smile and starts to talk in a kind of mangled Spanglish. I do not understand much of what he says, but I gather that it's somehow related to insects – or "eensex", as he calls them – because, he tells me, he hopes one day to become "an eensex-expert".

"An entomologist," I say.

"Yes! Yes!" He beams at the word. "So you like eensex too?"

I shake my head. His disappointment is clear.

We stand around, talking about moths and bugs, while drinking Coca-Cola from vintage glass bottles that we buy in one of the shacks. The supplies that

Lucho has been loading are almost all on board, and soon it will be our turn to be ferried across the water. I get ready to leave, but then I notice something disturbing. Over the shoulder of the budding entomologist, I see that the boats, which have carried supplies to the *Iguana*, are coming back empty – not just of the supplies, but also of the people who, I thought, were just milling around and helping.

And slowly it dawns on me. These people are not here to see us on our way – nor to talk about "eensex". They are here because they are coming *with* us. Every single one of them.

It takes me a while to get it straight, but as near as I can tell, this is the passenger list for the *Iguana*.

- Lucho, our guide.
- Natalia, his wife.
- Their baby – now known to be four months old.
- Camille – Lucho's and Natalia's other child, a three-year-old boy.
- Janet, the babysitter – a girl of about eighteen, who, a few days before, was hired by Lucho

and Natalia from the streets of Puerto
Ayacucho.
- An unnamed teenage boy – another of Lucho's
sons, from, I think, an earlier marriage.
- A woman named Betty, – who is Lucho's
sister-in-law.
- The day captain – who will steer the boat.
A back-up captain – who will steer the boat
while the day captain sleeps.
- Luis – one of the captain's sons, and an
obvious streetwise urchin.
- Linda – one of Lucho's sisters, who serves as
the *Iguana*'s main cook.
- Justa – a Venezuelan fish researcher.
- Another fish researcher – a colleague of Justa's,
whose name I never learn.
- Leopoldo – aka Leo   the would-be
entomologist, who is also Justa's son,
- An unidentified woman, who appears to be
hitching a ride up-river.
- Miriam.
- Me.

We leave Samariapo at 10.00 a.m. and head upstream with the current strong against us. I am no longer thinking, "**Here be Dragons**". Instead I am thinking, "**Here be People**". Lucho tells the day captain to stay close to the shore and avoid the main flow. As Samariapo disappears over the stern, the rain starts to fall in slanting, leaden sheets, drumming on the rear deck directly above us. The heat plasters our clothes against our skin as if we'd been drenched. We stay hunkered down, sheltering behind rolls of canvas that Lucho unfurls from the deck above, but when the clouds briefly part, we stick out our heads for a glimpse of the sun. The river slides past us like mercury. Normally chocolate brown, it now glints silver.

Well clear of the rapids, the Orinoco broadens out until it is three, even four, miles wide. It looks magnificent – full of energy and power, with swirling eddies close to the shore and a smooth-flowing current out near the centre. Incredibly, this massive river will begin to shrink when the rainy season ends, until, in about four months time, it will be little more than a trickle.

We stop briefly at Isla Ratón, the largest permanent island in the Orinoco. Its Spanish name sounds better than the English translation. Another cloud of rain sweeps in, but after it passes, I climb the short ladder to the rear deck and lay claim to a white plastic chair, which I position just aft of a clothes line and the army of oil drums that hold our spare fuel. With so many people on board, it's essential to commandeer some personal space. Everyone does so, with the exception of Leo, who crosses the many invisible boundaries to talk to anyone who'll listen about "eensex".

I wonder how Lucho managed to get the *Iguana* above the rapids, but of course, he didn't. The *Iguana* was built – about twenty years ago – in Manaus, so it came here by way of the Casiquiare.

Below me in the galley, I hear Linda preparing lunch – fish in turmeric, rice, fried plantains, black beans, papaya and melon juice. We eat in shifts on the lower deck – an open-sided area now that Lucho has rolled up the canvas sheets – which is almost exactly a table-length wide. It is clammy and hot, and soon the rain again lashes down, ruling out the possibility of further conversation.

That evening, I find myself unaccountably depressed. I think it might be because of the *Iguana* and its cheery primary colours. Or perhaps it's because of the food – there's far too much, and it's far too good. Or maybe it's because there's a baby on board, which helps to create an extended-family feel whenever a group of us gathers to eat. Whatever the reason, I feel I'm suffering from an acute lack of challenge. It's all too easy. It's all too soft. There is no privation. No suffering. This is not the stuff of explorers. This is not the way that Stanley would have travelled.

Later, as we squash into our tiny cabin, Miriam tries to console me. "Don't worry," she says, "From here on, I'm sure things can only get worse."

4

A Monstrous Error of Geography

Europeans first sighted the Orinoco in 1498, when Columbus – on his third voyage to the New World – sailed past its mouth. Columbus did not venture inland, but in the first half of the 16th century Spanish conquistadors sailed far up-river in their endless search for gold, and in 1595 Sir Walter Raleigh – founder of the first English colony in the Americas – fought his way three hundred miles upstream as part of *his* search for the elusive El Dorado. But if the Orinoco appealed to the Europeans' greed, it was a minor offshoot – the Casiquiare – that appealed to their sense of wonder. It was this river – a much smaller river that seemed to have no material value – which caught their attention and held them enthralled.

The Casiquiare story rightly begins in 1494, when Pope Alexander VI split the New World into two. Until that year, Portugal and Spain – then the two leading explorer-nations – had squabbled over which country could lawfully lay claim to the various lands that were just beginning to be discovered by Europeans. Like most popes of his time, Alexander – a member of the notorious Borgia family – was thoroughly corrupt, happy to bribe, steal, fornicate and murder his way to the top. But as head of the Roman Catholic Church, he ran the only transnational organization then in existence, so it was natural that the two countries should appeal to him for help in settling their dispute.

With the Treaty of Tordesillas, Alexander decreed that all land to the west of a line that ran north-south through the New World – some 370 leagues west of the Cape Verdes islands – should belong to Spain, while all land to the east of the line should belong to Portugal. This division clearly favoured Spain – Alexander was

Spanish-born, as well as being a friend of the Spanish king – but both parties came to embrace it.

Six years later, in 1500, a Portuguese navigator – Pedro Álvares Cabral – sailed down the west coast of Africa, but then, either by accident or design, he was blown so far off course that he crossed the Atlantic and discovered the land that later became Brazil. The coast Cabral sighted lay to the east of Alexander's line of demarcation, so Cabral claimed it in the name of his king, thereby giving Portugal a small foothold in the New World.

Both the Orinoco and Amazon basins lay well to the west of Alexander's line, so in the eyes of the Europeans, they fell under the sway of Spain. But Spain possessed so much territory in the New World that it could not develop it all, and over the next 150 years, it slowly lost its grip on most of the Amazon basin. This left Portugal free to expand its New World foothold until it could legitimately claim nearly all of the land that was drained by the world's greatest river. By the mid-17th century, the Orinoco remained a Spanish river. But the Amazon – along with its major tributaries – lay firmly in the hands of the Portuguese.

Nearly one hundred years later, in 1744, a Jesuit priest named Father Manuel Roman was paddling the upper reaches of the Orinoco – far above the Atures and Maipures rapids – when, to his astonishment, he came across a marauding band of Portuguese slave traders. How, he wondered, could Portuguese traders have made their way so far up what was indisputably a Spanish river? The slave traders gave him the answer when they led him even further up the Orinoco – and then down the Casiquiare to the settlements they had established on the Rio Negro. The Orinoco had a back door – a river that connected the Spanish and Portuguese lands.

Father Roman was not the first European to write about the Casiquiare. That distinction belongs to another Jesuit priest, Father Christóbal de Acuña, who had heard about the river more than one hundred years before, when he travelled the Amazon from its upper tributaries down to its mouth on the South Atlantic. But Father Roman became the first to paddle along the Casiquiare and to publish an account of his journey.

His report might have been ignored, but in 1745 it came to the attention of the French Académie des Sciences in Paris. And suddenly, all of Europe sat up and took notice.

‸

By the mid-18th century, Portugal and Spain had ceased to be the dominant nations in the field of exploration. That distinction now belonged to England and France. But while England sent expeditions around the world, intended to map specific lands, France, as befits a founding nation of the Enlightenment, set out to define the entire globe.

One question that particularly vexed the French concerned the shape of the Earth. Was it a perfect sphere – a view that was considered past its prime – or did it bulge out like an overweight *flâneur* at either the Poles or the Equator? That question was of more than academic interest. If the Earth was a sphere, then the length of the arc of a single degree would be the same wherever it was measured; but if, as most scientists believed, the Earth was distorted, then the length of the arc would vary with its location on the Earth's surface. The question therefore had profound significance for the way that sailors – and explorers – navigated their way around the world, and for the way they mapped any new lands they might happen to find.

The French Académie decided to settle the issue by sending an expedition west to Spanish Peru to measure the length of an arc near the Equator, while sending a second expedition north to Lapland to measure the length of an arc close to one of the poles. The two expeditions were expected to return at approximately the same time, but the Peruvian one had further to go, so it left first, in 1735. Nominally under the command of Louis Godin, the man who had proposed it, the expedition soon fell under the control of one of its more prominent members – a wealthy, distinguished scientist and explorer with the mellifluous name of Charles Marie de La Condamine.

Ten years passed before La Condamine returned to Paris. During that time, he suffered extreme hardship, and saw his expedition fall apart as its members quarrelled, died, fought, went mad and sued one another. But at least La Condamine had a result. He was able to report that the Earth was not a sphere, but did, in fact, bulge out – at the Equator. Unfortunately for La Condamine, the Lapland expedition had returned seven years earlier with much the same finding – so while La Condamine could claim to have made many discoveries, he was nonetheless cheated of the glory he felt he deserved.

"We returned seven years too late to inform Europe of anything new," he wrote gloomily in one report.

But worse was yet to come. Partly because he was no longer on speaking terms with the other expedition members, La Condamine returned to France by making an epic journey down the length of the Amazon, crossing the entire South American continent rather than taking the easy way around by ship. It was an astounding effort and a major feat of exploration, so when, in 1745, he gave an account of his travels to the Académie, he anticipated a warm and rapturous reception.

However, La Condamine knew of Father Roman's report of the Casiquiare, and while travelling along the

Amazon, he had himself heard stories of this strange river. When he announced to the Académie that the Casiquiare united the Orinoco and Amazon basins, he provoked uproar rather than applause. It was just too absurd, his audience hooted. Had La Condamine taken leave of his senses? Did he really believe the river flowed *over* its watershed? Was he seriously proposing that it ran *uphill*?

Much to his dismay, La Condamine found himself the target of unprecedented abuse. "This is not the first time that what is positive fact has been thought fabulous," he lamented. "But the spirit of criticism has been pushed too far."

For the next fifty-five years, the "Casiquiare question" bitterly divided the leading geographers of Europe. At times, tempers ran so high that bewigged, learned gentlemen were provoked to angry blows. The Spanish government attempted to calm the waters by sending several expeditions to see if the river even existed – let alone joined two river basins. But near the end of the 18th century, when the much-respected French geographer Philippe Buache drew a map of the

area, he pointedly excluded all signs of the Casiquiare – even adding an acerbic note at the bottom of his
map: "The long-supposed communication between
the Orinoco and the Amazon is a monstrous error of
geography."

It was not until 1800, when the Casiquiare was
properly explored by the Prussian naturalist Baron
Friedrich Heinrich Alexander von Humboldt and the
French botanist Aimé Bonpland, that the unique character of the river was finally accepted. Humboldt hated
the Casiquiare, calling it "the most painful part of my
travels in America", but he paddled the river from one
end to the other and proved once and for all that it did
indeed unite the Orinoco and the Amazon basins.

Unfortunately, Humboldt failed to explain just
how the Casiquiare performed this remarkable feat – a
failure that created as much confusion as he had tried
to clear up.

5

Learning Much from the "Eensex"

It's early morning, and I'm on the rear deck, sticking uncomfortably to my plastic chair, half hidden behind a cordon of oil drums and a semaphore of shirts, underpants and towels that are attached by wooden pegs to the clothesline. I can see Luis, the captain's son, taunting a butterfly near the bow by the wheelhouse, as well as the metronomic swing of Janet's – the babysitter's – bare feet as she rocks back and forth on a hammock one deck below.

I'm reading a vivid account of Stanley's epic search for Livingstone, which, I know, is an inappropriately landlocked book to bring on a river trip, but I want to re-read Stanley's account of his adventures and see how mine might begin to compare. Stanley has been commissioned by James Gordon Bennett, Jr., the owner, editor and publisher of the *New York Herald* – a "three-cent scandal sheet", as it's been called – to journey into the heart of Africa and find Livingstone, who has been "lost" somewhere in the middle of that continent for the past five years.

Stanley's commission is considerably grander than mine – and better funded, too. He claims, somewhat improbably, that he has been financed with a US$20,000 line of credit – more than ten times the amount that I've received *without* adjusting for inflation. He has just left Zanzibar – on February 5, 1871 – and is fighting his way inland, travelling with a couple of drunken English sailors, the only Europeans he could persuade to accompany him, and nearly two hundred locally hired soldiers and porters, who are loaded down with more than eight *tons* of beads, wire, cloth, food, candles, medicines, tents, personal gear, ammunition, two dismantled boats, and a substantial arsenal of "one double-barrel, breech-loading smooth bore gun; one

American Winchester rifle, or sixteen-shooter; two Starr's breech-loaders; one Jocelyn breech-loader; one elephant rifle; two breech-loading revolvers; twenty-four muskets, or flint locks; six single-barreled pistols; one battle axe; two swords; two daggers; one boar spear; two American axes; twenty-four hatchets; and twenty-four butcher knives."

As Stanley begins to hack his way through the coastal jungle, I am joined on the deck of the *Iguana* by Leo, the entomologist, who has tracked me down and is now standing beside me, holding a butterfly net the size of a windsock. This, along with his outfit of khaki shirt and baggy pants, gives him the timely look of a 19th-century explorer. Leo, I've learned, will not leave me alone, but keeps invading my space behind the oil drums and clothesline to talk – inevitably – about "eensex". He should be annoying, but the raw enthusiasm he shows for his obsession makes him somehow endearing.

He gives me a brief lecture about the number of "eensex" species there are in this world.

"And we keep finding more," he says.

I tell him that perhaps we should leave them unfound, since 99.99 percent of all the species we've ever discovered are now extinct.

"No, no," he says, "it is we who will one day go extinct. We've been here only a short time and already we can kill ourselves many times over. But the eensex – they are smarter. They will go on forever. We have much to learn," he says, "from the eensex."

I'm trying to think of a suitable response when the boat suddenly lurches. It throws Leo off balance and nearly dumps me out of my chair. I think for a moment that we have hit something lurking in the water, but I look around and see that a military patrol boat, bristling with guns, has snuck up alongside us, rocking the *Iguana* in its wash. A crew of heavily armed teenagers – kitted out in boots, gaiters, cargo pants, camouflage tee-shirts and wrap-around shades – glares down at us from its deck. The gun-boat edges closer, cuts its engines, and an officer on board gestures for us to do the same.

Six of the teenagers swing over the railings and land on our deck. They all have baby-smooth cheeks and rifles that they keep at the ready, and they are backed up by a fixed machine-gun set aft of the turret on their patrol boat. It's a scene from *Apocalypse Now*, and I half expect to hear Wagner's *Ride of the Valkyries* blare out from loudspeakers. The soldiers fan out, poking their rifles into cabins and demanding to see papers and identity cards, then search the hold, down near the engines. One of them counts the oil drums, pointing at each one like a teacher taking roll-call. He says nothing to me.

Ten minutes later, the teenagers are back on the gun-boat, their faces still masks, eyes shielded by their shades. Their engines fire and they peel away, leaving us rocking and rolling in their wake.

I look for Lucho. He shrugs. "The National Guard," he says. "Just checking for gasoline. And making sure it's not being smuggled."

Gun-boat inspections are common along this stretch of the Orinoco, he tells me, since the river here forms the border between Venezuela on the east and Colombia on the west. The cocaine that comes out of Colombia is often paid for by gasoline smuggled in from Venezuela.

For the most part, Lucho says, the trafficking is controlled by FARC – a Spanish acronym for the Revolutionary Armed Forces of Colombia – which is a narco-terrorist organization that once was a left-wing guerilla group with political goals, but in the past twenty years has morphed into a criminal gang that trades not just in drugs and gasoline, but also in gold and people. It now claims some 20,000 "members", many of them recruited by force, which allows it to dominate as much as one-third of Colombia – an area the size of Switzerland – primarily along the lawless borders that Colombia shares with Venezuela, Brazil and Peru.

More recently, FARC has branched out into hijacking, extortion and kidnapping, running up huge profits that, more often than not, are laundered through American banks. Failure to pay a FARC demand almost always results in death for the victim, but immediate payment is often followed by further demands – and then by the dumping of a bullet-ridden body.

↩

At Castillito, we visit our first Indian village. It's a Curripaco village, Lucho informs us, although the indigenous name for the Curripaco tribe is "Wakuénai". That means the people here speak Wakú, which, he says, is part of the Arawak family of languages.

Lucho does not offer this information. Instead, we have to winkle it out of him with a series of questions framed in devious ways. It is clear that he knows the river and understands the people who live on its banks, so he should be an excellent guide – he *is* an excellent guide – but he keeps his knowledge bottled up inside him as if he's afraid that letting it out will somehow destroy it.

He beckons us into a hut that is wedged between an oil drum and a banana tree. When our eyes adjust to the gloom, we see an Indian woman squatting down and peeling yucca with a serious machete that she wields like a broad-sword. The yucca, Lucho grudgingly reveals, is a kind of tuber, like a potato. The Indians grind it down, force it through a strainer, or *sebucán*, to extract its liquids, then mix it with water and bake it into a hard, flat bread, called *casabe*.

Casabe is one of the mainstays of the Curripaco

diet, and is prepared only by the women, who must grow, gather, peel, grind and press the yucca, as well as collect the firewood that's needed to bake it. They must also get every step in the process right – especially the pressing – because the yucca the Indians use is highly toxic. The liquid that's extracted is, in fact, a form of cyanide, which, in sufficient doses, can be deadly. Sometimes, Lucho tells us, it is used to poison the tips of darts and arrows that the Indians use for hunting.

Squeezing these facts out of Lucho is harder than straining the acid out of a yucca, but outside the hut, he offers some information without any prompting. The banana tree that grows by the entrance is not native, he says. Banana trees may have been in the area a long time – perhaps for as long as two hundred years – but they originally came from Indonesia.

Lucho, it seems, feels secure about bananas.

⌐

Our next stop is San Fernando de Atabapo, a hot apology of a town that until the 1900s, when a road reached Puerto Ayacucho, was the capital of Venezuela's Amazonas state. It's in decline now, but at the start of the last century, it was a rip-roaring, wide-open place reminiscent of Dodge or Leadville in their heyday in the American west. For many years, the city fell under the sway of one Tomás Funes, the last of a long line of rubber – or robber – barons, who abused the local people and turned many of them into slaves. Funes seized power after murdering the state governor, then tried to make a fortune by selling egret feathers, which at that time were in high demand in the fashionable salons of Europe. When that venture faltered, he took control of the rubber industry, boosting his power to such an extent that the national government in Caracas felt its rule over the state, the country's largest, was under terminal threat. In the 1930s, Funes was forcibly deposed and executed in the town's main square.

We visit the site – an unmarked wisp of grass, overlooked by a town hall that rises in steps like tiers on a wedding-cake.

Near the dock, Leo finds a small scorpion, which he swings by the tail in front of my face.

"It is deadly," he says.

I think he's exaggerating, just trying to scare me. But I'm not entirely sure.

↵

It was here in San Fernando that Alexander von Humboldt – on his journey up the Orinoco – left the river and headed south to travel along the Atabapo as far as the Temi. He made a short, but arduous, portage to the Guiania, and followed that river downstream as far as the Rio Negro. He then paddled up the Casiquiare to rejoin the Orinoco, which he descended until he arrived back at San Fernando.

I don't know much about Humboldt, even though he has, at times, been lumped with Goethe, Kant and Schiller, and praised as "the first ecologist, a proto-Transcendentalist, who influenced Poe, Emerson, the Hudson River School painters, and a host of scientists and explorers". My ignorance stems mainly from the fact that Humboldt, although Prussian, is now presented as German, and growing up as I did in the shadow of the

Second World War, we did not "do" Germans – even good ones. But for five years, from 1799 to 1804, Humboldt explored much of South America.

In large part, Humboldt was inspired by La Condamine's accounts of his various travels, and when he and his companion Bonpland arrived in South America, they were determined to experience as much of the new continent as they could. Both men – Humboldt and Bonpland – were delighted with the novelty that South America represented, and they behaved, at first, like spoiled children with too many toys.

"We were always leaving one object to throw it away for another," Humboldt wrote.

In April 1801, Humboldt was in Colombia, where he explored the Magdalena River and then crossed the Andes by horseback to reach Bogotá. In September, he headed for Ecuador, where he tried to climb that country's highest peak – the 20,561-foot Mount Chimborazo – reaching 19,286 feet, the highest that anyone had ever climbed, before altitude sickness forced him to turn back.

He then made an epic, 1,000-mile journey down the

line of the Andes as far as Lima. The last six hundred miles of this trip took him along Peru's coastal plain, allowing him to observe and chart the cool, off-shore current that now bears his name. After several months in Lima, he set sail for Mexico and Cuba, and finally fetched up in the United States. There he was honoured and feted, and introduced to Thomas Jefferson, the American president, who had just waved goodbye to Lewis and Clark on *their* expedition to explore the lands west of the Mississippi – lands that America had recently acquired from France under the Louisiana Purchase.

～

For our part, when we leave San Fernando, we make a sharp left turn. We're no longer following the border with Colombia, but continue up the Orinoco, still fighting its strong current by keeping near to the shore. The jungle closes in like the covers of a book, and more rain falls out of a gray, glowering sky. Miriam and I head for our cabin and climb into our bunks, lying on thin, clammy sheets. We each have a mosquito net we've nailed into place, as well as a shared fan that we've started to fight over.

With the aid of a head torch, I read that Stanley, too, is constantly being plagued by heat and humidity.

"The atmosphere, pent in by the density of the jungle, was hot and stifling," he writes. "The perspiration transuded through every pore."

Sometime during the night, I slide out of my bunk and take an Orinoco-river shower in one of the toilet stalls at the stern. It cools me down – for a moment at least – but in the hot, saturated air, the effect doesn't linger.

Back in the cabin, I find that the captain has docked by ramming the *Iguana*'s bow into the jungle. A branch like a triffid pokes through the open hatch that passes for a porthole. It has small sharp thorns on it, as well as a parasitic vine. I lie down again, the air so thick I can barely breathe, while my sweat – like Stanley's – transudes through every pore.

6

A Waif-like Figure On Board

The *Iguana* tows two small boats in its wake – a wooden rowing-boat and a much larger, aluminium motor boat. Today, we take the motor boat – the so-called *voladora*, or "fast boat" – and head for Cárida, an illegal, gold-mining camp on the west bank of the river.

I've always had a romanticized view of gold-mining camps, especially illegal ones. I picture them as vibrant, brawling places that may be as corrupt as the US Senate, but at least they spill over with vigour and life. The reality, it turns out, is considerably different – at least in Cárida.

As Lucho nudges the fast boat close to the shore, we see a ramshackle collection of tumbledown huts. He stops by a single wooden board that serves as a dock and we tightrope-walk our way onto dry land, arms extended for balance. The huts, up-close, appear to have been slammed together from rough-hewn planks with sheets of corrugated iron nailed on top. In front of one of them, a group of women stand ankle-deep in mud, sheltering beneath a spread tarpaulin and trying to cook over a logwood fire they have lit in an oil-drum lid. As we walk by, we feel the crawl of hostile eyes across our faces. The few men we come across are falling-down drunk, and in several of the huts we see prostitutes lying prone on wooden pallets, too listless to come to the door and tout for trade.

We enter one of the huts to meet a couple of Lucho's friends. Two women are hunkered down on the dirt floor. One of them looks middle-aged, old before her time. The other is young and strikingly attractive – much too attractive for her own good.

"Beautiful, no?" Lucho says.

Miriam crouches beside them to talk. Every day,

the women tell her, they paddle across the Orinoco to the Yapacana Cerro National Park. Everyone does – all the people in the camp who still harbour hope. The Park is a protected area, one of four in Amazonas state, and in theory at least, only qualified scientists working on officially approved projects are entitled to enter. In practice, the Park is centred on a *cerro*, or hill, which contains a smattering of gold. So every day, it swarms with illegal miners from the Cárida camp.

The Venezuelan National Guard is supposed to drive the miners away, and there's a guard post we passed just a few miles down-river. The women smile when we mention this. The National Guard is easily bought, they say, and Cárida is well-entrenched. The older of the women was born in this camp – and she is second generation.

With some coaxing from Lucho, the younger woman produces a small, black box, which she opens to reveal a tiny nugget wrapped in cloth. She shows it to us, holding it up to the light from the door so we see it sparkle and glitter. The nugget might be worth one hundred American dollars, she says – maybe a little more. She smiles as she looks at it, and for a moment she is in some other place. Then she wraps the nugget up and carefully settles it in its black box. She needs to hide it from the menfolk, she says, to make sure they don't drink it away or, worse still, blow it on the prostitutes next door.

~

Back on board the *Iguana*, I make a surprise discovery. At San Fernando, we said goodbye to Betty, Lucho's sister-in-law, who left the boat there, along with the woman who was hitching a ride. That left fifteen people on board. As I settle once more into my chair, I know without checking that Natalia will be in her cabin with the baby; Linda, the cook, will be in the galley; Camille will be running around below; Lucho will be down by the engines; and Leo will be checking the pinning-boards of "eensex" that, he has told me, he stores under his bunk. Even so, it's hard to keep track of where everyone is, so it takes me some time to realize that someone new is on board – a strange, waif-like figure I see flitting across the fore deck like a shadow.

I go down to the engines to search out Lucho. Yes, he tells me, we've taken on another passenger – one we picked up at Bella Vista, where we briefly stopped to trade for supplies. He's an Indian, Lucho says, making his way up river, so we've offered him a lift – up the Orinoco and part of the way along the Casiquiare. I nod and go back to my plastic chair, intrigued and alert, because the new arrival is, as I suspected, a member of that much-anticipated, belligerent tribe – the dreaded Yanomami.

7

Naked and High on Yopo

One of the first Westerners to encounter the Yanomami was an American anthropologist named Napoleon Chagnon, who stumbled upon a nomadic tribe in the early 1960s. This is what he had to say about them:

"I looked up and gasped, when I saw a dozen burly, naked, filthy, hideous men staring at us down the shafts of their drawn arrows. Immense wads of green tobacco were stuck between their lower teeth and lips, making them look even more hideous, and strands of dark-green slime dripped or hung from their noses."

The Yanomami are not an attractive people – at

least not to Western eyes. I cannot claim to know everything about them, but I do know that the men traditionally go naked except for a single cotton string, which they tie around their waists. This string loops down from their waists and attaches to their drawn-out foreskins and is then pulled up tight so that their penises are held flat against their bellies in a kind of flaccid erection. As a rule, the men also sport livid scars, since most disputes – even between members of the same village – are settled by the opponents standing toe-to-toe and pounding each other over the head with staves. The scars the combatants inflict can last a lifetime, but since they are worn with considerable pride, they are often exhibited by shaving off the hair that surrounds them or enhanced by highlighting them with a blood-red pigment.

On festive occasions, the men are known to decorate themselves with headdresses and armbands of parrot or curassow feathers, but when they go on raids, they usually paint themselves black to mimic the colour of night and to represent death. When they wish to relax – or communicate with the spirit world

– they like to blow a strong hallucinogenic drug up one another's nostrils using a three-foot-long tube called a *mokohiro*. Their drug of choice is *yopo*, which is made from the powdered, inner bark of the *yakowana* tree mixed in human saliva. By all accounts, *yopo* gives its users a monumental high as well as an excruciating headache. It also produces the dark-green slime that hangs from their noses, which Chagnon couldn't help but notice during his first encounter.

As for the women, they too paint their faces and bodies, but they also decorate themselves with facial sticks that pierce their noses, cheeks and lips. This arrangement of sticks is apparently an attempt to imitate the whiskers of a jaguar, but at first sight it can look as if the women have been shot in the face by arrows. As a general rule, the women go bare-breasted, their upper bodies covered only by a woven strap that winds around their necks and seats a baby or two on the sides of their hips. They start to bear children at a very young age, and nurse each one for several years, so by the time they reach twenty, their bodies appear slack and overly-used.

The women, too, are frequently marked by scars – which, more often than not, have been inflicted during beatings administered by the men – and almost all of them have, at one time or another, been the victims of rape.

Both sexes have straight, jet-black hair, customarily cut in a pudding-basin style. And physically, they are muscular, quick and strong. Their staple diet consists of plants that have a high calorie-count, as well as meat and fish when they can get it. For the most part, they have just enough to eat, but it's not always what they would like. As a result, the Yanomami have two distinct words for hunger. One means, "I have an empty stomach"; while the other means, "I have a *full* stomach – but I crave meat".

↜

I know one other thing about the Yanomami, and that too, relates to their vocabulary.

Several years ago, I attended a lecture on language and what it tells you about the cultures that developed it. The speaker maintained that common words and expressions reveal much more than might at first be apparent.

For example, the French have an expression, *faire le pont*, which literally means "to make the bridge". There is no concise, English equivalent, but, roughly translated, it means that if, in France, a national holiday falls on a Thursday, then the entire country will "make the bridge" by taking off the Friday, too, thus creating a four-day break out of what otherwise would be a normal weekend. What this tells you, if you didn't already know it, is that the French don't particularly like to work.

On Easter Island, the locals have a word, *tingo*, which broadly means "to borrow things from a friend's house, one by one, until there is nothing left worth taking." Entire books have been written about Easter Island and why the culture there collapsed, but this one word – all by itself – tells you everything you need to know.

In Iraq, there's a word, *sahel*, which George W. Bush might have learned had he taken the time to perceive the distinction between Sunnis and Shias before he invaded their country. It basically means "to defeat your enemy to the point where he's humiliated, and then drag his body through the streets." With a word like that in the Iraqi lexicon, it should have been clear to anyone who looked that the country nurtured a vengeful society that could easily slide into civil war.

As for the Yanomami, they have a word, *nomohoni*, which also has no simple, English equivalent, but it generally means "to employ trickery in order to set up a massacre." This can be a complex concept to incorporate into a single word, and most cultures don't need it. But the Yanomami find that the word gives them a convenient, short-hand way to describe a series of events by which one tribe fools another into placing itself in a vulnerable position and then slaughters it.

What this one word tells you is that the Yanomami can be devious – and that they richly deserve their reputation for ferocity and violence.

꒰

But maybe not.

It doesn't take long, even when conducting the most cursory research on the Yanomami, to find that nearly everything about them is steeped in controversy – including their much-touted reputation for violence and aggression.

The arguments began with Napoleon Chagnon's work in the 1960s and the publication in 1968 of his best-selling book, *Yanomamo*, in which he dwelt extensively on the high levels of aggression he said he observed among the Yanomami – describing, for example, how arguments between rival groups rapidly escalate from initial chest thumping, to chest pounding with rocks, to side slapping, then to club and spear fighting, and finally to premeditated killing during ambushes and raids.

Subtitling his book *The Fierce People* helped underline this apparent belligerence – and so, too, did his report in the February 26, 1988, edition of the magazine, *Science*, in which he said, almost in passing, that nearly one-third of Yanomami men could be expected to suffer a violent death, and nearly one-half were guilty of what we would term murder. As Chagnon himself said, his work finally put an end to the automatic reverence and respect with which primitive people were regarded, because at long last he had managed to debunk "all that crap about the Noble Savage."

However, in 2000 an investigative journalist named Patrick Tierney published a much fatter book, *Darkness in Eldorado*, in which – among other even more serious matters – he challenged the foundation of Chagnon's methods and data. In particular, Tierney claimed that Chagnon had provoked the Indians by offering gifts to any tribe that helped him with his research. This created such high levels of competition and resentment, Tierney maintained, that Chagnon himself was the instigator of much of the violence he claimed merely to have observed.

After Tierney's book was published, the American Anthropological Association formed a special committee to investigate all of the author's allegations, and in 2002, it released a 304-page report that cleared Chagnon of many of the crimes of which he'd been accused – but found him guilty of others. Three years later, in a further twist, the Association reversed course and voted to reject its earlier report, because, it said, its special committee had been excessively biased.

And there the matter rests, at least for the moment, leaving the anthropologists to bubble and boil with their own brand of violence and aggression – so much so that if the Yanomami hadn't already done so, they would, no doubt, have coined their own term for the word "*nomohoni*".

～

Before embarking on this journey, Miriam and I visited our local, university library to see some movies – filmed, for the most part, in the 1970s and 1990s – which showed the Yanomami in their natural setting. The figures we watched were surreal, bizarre. The men crawled around in a *yopo*-fueled stupor, naked and painted, with their lower lips stretched and distorted by hockey-puck wedges of dried tobacco they had stuffed into their mouths; while the women sat in groups, picking lice and nits out of one another's hair.

They were more than primitive. They were crude and alien. Mythical people from another world.

On the *Iguana* – from my secure position behind the oil drums – I can observe the Yanomami man we have taken on board. He does not look drugged. Nor does he does seem unduly violent or aggressive. If anything, he appears physically fragile, as if he's deflated – perhaps even depressed. He is not at all like the "burly, filthy, hideous men" that Chagnon saw. Instead, he's an undersized figure, twig-like and small, with eyes set deep in a gaunt face. He's dressed only in a torn and dirty tee-shirt, his dark, sinewy neck poking out of the top like a ventriloquist's dummy's. I don't think he has tied up his penis, but when he moves across the deck, I can see that his testicles are dangling down like a couple of Maltesers.

Most of the time, he squats on the fore deck – peering into the jungle with a glazed, almost blank expression – but his primary base is one level down near the cooler, just outside Linda's galley. That's where he has secreted a small plastic bag that appears to contain his worldly possessions. There is a warm spot on the floor where the cooler dissipates heat, and he spends his nights there, curled up on the rough boards – although why he seeks heat in *this* climate, I cannot begin to understand.

I do not know the man's name, but I have learned from Lucho that the Yanomami are usually named for their relevant, kinship ties – "brother", "sister", "father", "mother". I do not, of course, share any of these relationships with him, so for the want of anything better, I decide for the moment to call him "Y".

8

*Men from Moon,
Women from Wabu*

When I look up at the night sky, I think I see a Universe that was created nearly fourteen billion years ago – one that started with a Big Bang, which was not a spectacular explosion as its name implies, but was, rather, a quantum event of unknown probability that involved the sudden expansion of a singularity, within which all the matter, energy and space in the Universe was contained. It is my belief that during this period of rapid expansion – lasting for just the tiniest fraction of a second – the Universe ballooned massively in size; the initial symmetry was distorted; and, as a result, some matter was able to survive, rather than be wiped out by its nemesis, anti-matter, which then existed in very nearly the same amount.

Later – much later – some of the surviving matter coalesced into stars and planets; and on at least one of those planets, the one we call Earth, life was somehow created – perhaps when a mix of organic chemicals, swirling around in a primordial pool, became intricate enough to reproduce. No one really knows. Certainly I don't. But once life got underway, evolution kicked in, and those early life-forms developed into something much more complex, which now includes me.

In the future, I believe that the Universe will continue to expand at a rate that, surprisingly, is accelerating rather than slowing down – driven by a mysterious, Star Wars force, which no one yet understands, called "dark energy". Eventually, the Universe will become a cold and lonely place, which from all points of view – if anyone, or anything, is still around to observe it – will appear empty and dead. By that time, of course, our Sun will have long ago died and all life on Earth will have ceased.

That's my creation story, the one I carry around in

my head. I do not know if all of it's true – or even if there's such a thing as an objective truth – but that is the way I view the Universe and the way it came to be.

～

From my chair behind the oil drums, I look across at Y on the foredeck. He has risen from his normal squat-position and now leans on the rail, gazing out at the jungle, much as I have been doing for the past several days. I am sure that Y knows nothing about my creation story, but I know a little about his. The Yanomami have different versions of how they came into this world, but if Y is a mainstream, conformist believer, then the chances are that his creation myth goes something like this.

Since the beginning of time, the Universe has consisted of four solid disks that are stacked one on top of the other like the layers of a cake. The uppermost layer stands empty, but it once contained all the living things that now reside in the other three layers. The second layer down is the sky layer, and it houses the departed souls that once lived on the third layer down, which is the Earth. This third layer down was formed when part of the sky layer fell off and dropped to a lower level.

Finally, there is a fourth, or bottom, layer. It, too, was once part of the sky layer and was formed when a chunk of the sky layer fell off; but this piece, when it broke away, fell through the Earth layer and kept on going. In the process, it took with it the inhabitants of one unfortunate Earth village, who were swept down to the bottom layer. These inhabitants continue to exist – but as spirit men, not real men. The spirit men are able to grow their own food, but they are not able to hunt. As a result, they are constantly hungry for game, so from time to time, they sneak up to the Earth layer, where they steal – and then eat – the souls of children.

As for life on Earth, it was created at the same time as the four-layered cosmos, beginning with strange beings who were part-men and part-spirits. These beings did not last long, since nearly all of them were drowned in a massive flood, but one of them – the spirit of the moon – managed to survive and came to live near, or hover over, a village of Earth inhabitants.

The people of the village hated the moon, because it would sometimes descend and, like the spirit men in the bottom layer of the cosmos, eat the souls of children. Specifically, the moon would place the souls between slices of *casabe* in what can only be described as a supernatural sandwich.

One day, an angry villager shot the moon with an arrow, and the moon's blood cascaded over the Earth, creating men – Yanomami men – who were thus, quite literally, born from blood. For a time, the men were happy. But they did not have any women until, one day, a group of men, out in the jungle, spotted a *wabu* fruit growing on a vine. When one of the men threw the fruit to the ground, it morphed into a woman, who happened to possess a particularly large and hairy vagina. All the men immediately had sex with this woman, then escorted her to their village where all the other men had sex with her, too.

And so began the Yanomami race.

∽

In many ways, I like Y's creation story better than mine. My cosmos is remote and impersonal – far too big to relate to, or even to imagine, let alone observe and understand. His is all around him, reassuringly close and providing a sense of where he belongs. At the same time, his knowledge of how life began – men from the moon and women from the *wabu* – means he can look around and literally *see* where he is from. He can also peer up at the sky – at the bottom of the second layer in his four-layer cosmos – and not only know that it definitely exists, but also know that that is where he is headed after death.

I can't do that. I'm forever cut off from my chemical origins; and I am not, as Y is, a single being whose spirit will survive after death, but am instead a temporary construct that has come together for a fleeting moment and will all too soon disperse. Like everyone else on this planet, I am made of billions of billions of atoms, each of which consists almost entirely of empty space. Most of these atoms – the hydrogen ones – were formed within the first micro-second of the Universe's creation, so they are nearly fourteen billion years old.

The other atoms – the heavier ones that are further up the periodic table – were all formed in stars that later exploded, spewing the atoms into space.

These other atoms are not as old as the hydrogen ones, but they, too, have spent billions of years travelling the Universe. I don't know where they have been, but I do know that they've spent time in many stars in the Milky Way or in other galaxies that I will never see. They have also spent time in other people, since all of us on Earth share atoms that once were part of Alexander the Great, Jesus Christ, Attila the Hun, Genghis Khan, Joan of Arc, and any number of other, more obscure human beings who have left no mark on history – not to mention the millions of plants and animals that my atoms have also passed through on their way to me. Some of these atoms were also once an integral part of Stanley at the same time that others were lodging in Livingstone – so they've already met before, on the shores of Lake Tanganyika in Africa. "Dr. Livingstone, I presume."

Somehow, enough of these atoms were scooped up to form the fetus that used to be me. But now, when I look at myself in the mirror, I no longer see any of these atoms, because as I grew up and then aged, I replaced every one of them with other atoms I picked up on the way. Like every other human being, I am, quite literally, no longer the person I was. And yet I can remember what I was like. *And* I can remember events from the past – events that took place *before* the atoms that now form me came to be me.

I find this disturbing, in a way that I'm sure Y never dreams of – because the events from my past are stored in atoms of my brain that were not there to record the events that they remember. My memory extends further back in time than I do. It predates me. And that makes me feel I have only a tenuous grip on reality. It also makes me wonder what exactly constitutes the "me" that is me.

One day, of course, I will surrender my atoms to other people, just as everyone else has done in the past. The atoms will live on, although I will not. I'm grateful for that, and I'm grateful to them. I'm thankful that in their endless wanderings throughout the Universe, they took the time briefly to form me. At the same time, I have to acknowledge that although those atoms are now within me, they are, nonetheless, only borrowed.

> While I am alive,
> I try to survive
> In bookstores, libraries and bars.
> But when I am dead,
> You'll find me instead,
> Adrift like dust in the stars.

9

As American as Casabe Pie

We get a chance, Y and I, to test our competing creation stories when we stop at the tiny settlement of Tamatama. Lucho tells us there's a mission there – a Christian one, run by Evangelicals, or born-again Christians. As we approach, he says that Miriam and I will feel at home in Tamatama, because the settlement is a little piece of middle America, located right here in the heart of the jungle. Also, an American lives there – a missionary, who is known to Lucho only as "Frank".

It turns out that Lucho doesn't much like Frank. But then, as we've discovered, Lucho doesn't seem to like *any* outsiders – especially those who, in his view, seek to meddle or interfere. Lucho likes to travel the river, shooting the breeze with the local people he knows and meets along the way. He enjoys his life, with its easy-going, free-wheeling style. He doesn't want to settle down and shop in a local market or store – he prefers to hunt, fish and forage. He's not damaging the environment, he says; he's not crazy enough to destroy his own way of life.

Yet there are people in the United States – and at the United Nations – who seem determined to change the way he lives. These people – these outsiders – think they know what's best, not just for him, but also for the jungle and indeed for all of Amazonas state. They want to save the trees, to save the Indians. They want to preserve and protect. But what do they know? Lucho says. He is an Indian, and this is *his* land. With their endless reports, the outsiders consume more trees than he'll ever cut down in a lifetime of plying the river, and they'll do far more harm to the indigenous people. The missionaries are the worst, he says, because they deliberately set out to undermine and destroy the native way of life. They should all go home – back to America, where they belong.

For Lucho, this is something of a rant.

༄

Understandably, Frank does not see things Lucho's way – not when Miriam and I clamber ashore and finally meet him. Frank sets his own agenda – one that is based on a creation myth, which is as fundamentally different from mine as it is from Y's. Frank's story, if I understand it correctly, begins on October 23, 4004 B.C., when God – a three-part being comprising God the Father, God the Son, and God the Holy Ghost – began his creation of the Earth and all living things in a burst of energy that lasted six days.

Then, on the final day, he scooped up a handful of dust and formed a man, Adam, and from one of Adam's ribs, he shaped a woman, Eve. He then set them in a paradise called Eden, where, in their innocence, they did not know they were naked until, at the urging of the Devil, in the shape of a snake, Eve ate an apple from the Tree of Knowledge of Good and Evil, which God had planted but had forbidden either Adam or Eve to touch. Eve offered the apple to Adam, and when he accepted, their spirits died.

When God asked Adam why he had eaten the fruit, Adam blamed Eve, who in turn blamed the snake, but by this time, both Adam and Eve were so ashamed of their nakedness that they covered their genitals – and possibly Eve's breasts – with fig-leaves. But the fig-leaves were too small for the job, so God killed an animal so they could use its skin for clothes, and in this way, Adam and Eve introduced not just sex into this world but also murder, so from that point on, all living creatures were destined to die. God knew, of course, that other people, once they came along, might reject him, so he planned to send his own Jesus Christ, to Earth in the full knowledge that Jesus would be asked to give up his life in exchange for universal forgiveness for all the sins of all the people for all time – but only if the people believed in him.

I have visions of Frank, Y and me putting our respective creation stories to a test – like playing a game of scissors, paper and stone – to see which one can vanquish the other two. But, of course, that doesn't happen. For one thing, Y stays on board the *Iguana*, and does not join us in Tamatama. This doesn't really surprise me, but the thought occurs to me – briefly and perhaps unkindly – that for someone who, until recently, has never seen the outside world, Y shows a remarkable lack of curiosity. But then, I think, he might just be in shock.

I well remember the trauma I suffered when, as a child, I moved from England to Scotland, and was forced to exchange mellow, yellow Bath stone for harsh granite and the books of S'r W'lt'r Sc'tt. I cannot imagine how much worse Y must feel. He is, I've discovered, on his way back from a trip down the Orinoco as far as Puerto Ayacucho, so in the past few days – for the first time in his life, and all in one sudden rush – he has been introduced to cars, telephones, shoes, beds, watches, electric lights, newspapers, televisions, buildings with doors in them, and water that flows out of taps. Still to come are hedge funds, derivatives, lap-tops, Blackberries, skate-shoes, tooth-bleach, cell phones, Moosehead beer, barbecues, Häagen-Dazs ice cream – and all the other indispensable trappings of our modern civilization.

At one point, back on the *Iguana*, I was tempted to show Y my iPod – putting the plugs into his ears and letting him listen to some of my music. But what would he have made of *Roll Over Beethoven*? Of *Heartbreak Hotel*? What would he have thought of *Tutti Frutti*?

> Got a gal named Sue
> She knows just what to do
> Tutti, frutti, aw, rutti,
> Awop bop a loo mop alop boom bam

～

As Miriam and I scramble up the mud bank that leads to Tainatama, we expect to enter the mini-America that Lucho promised. Instead, what we find only confirms that Lucho has never visited the United States.

Frank moves slowly as he shows us around, since the three of us are all visibly wilting in the heat. He points out buildings that are neater than those we have seen elsewhere – better constructed, and made of non-native materials, like stone and cement. He shows us the soccer pitch, the school and the church – a low building, painted white, with a sloped, corrugated-iron roof. Inside, ready for converts, are four rows of wooden pews, set in front of a rickety table with burned-out candles on top that serves as an altar; while outside, someone has made a vain attempt to hold back the jungle and replace it with a kind of manicured grass – an attempt, perhaps, to show just who's in charge here.

Frank himself is a stocky, sandy-haired man with a face ruddied by heat. He was born about forty years ago in upper New York State, but moved to Tamatama with his missionary family when he was nine. Now, he lives here with his brother, his brother's family, and two pilots who make dangerous use of the settlement's bumpy, truncated landing-strip to fly in food and other supplies. Frank is proud of what the mission has accomplished, and tells us about the Indian children who have passed through the school, as well as the two local doctors the mission has helped to train.

Christian missionaries have worked among the Yanomami for more than forty years, he tells us, and while they've made "progress", they have been never been entirely welcomed. Like Lucho, the Venezuelan government suspects their motives. At times, it has accused the missionaries of spying for foreign interests: the CIA, mining conglomerates, and pharmaceuticals firms that want to test drugs on indigenous peoples. The government also accuses the missionaries of destroying cultural beliefs, and, with their many competing and conflicting Christian doctrines, of sowing the seeds of cultural confusion.

Frank rejects these charges when I gently put them to him, and instead echoes the Pope's recent claim that the native people of the New World were crying out for salvation when the Europeans arrived and gave them smallpox. Part of me would like to tell Frank that his three-part God, with his dust man and rib-woman, means no more to me than Y's four-tier Universe with its moon-man and *wabu*-woman. Certainly, it would be nice to have some kind of god looking out for my interests – helping me find a job, make an important speech, or just turn the traffic lights green whenever I'm running late for an appointment. But try as I might, I find it hard to believe in something for which there's no evidence. I don't ask for proof (although I sometimes see a red traffic light as a clear sign that God does *not* exist). I'd be willing to accept a nudge and a wink. But lacking even that, I am forced to conclude that God did not make Man in his own image, but rather that Man made God in *his* own image – or as Voltaire once said: "If God didn't exist, then Man would have invented him".

I would be happy to have a discussion about this with Frank. But of course, it's not possible to reason your way towards God, and anyway, I am constrained by the rules of my culture, which say that, on first meeting, you do not attack another person's core beliefs, especially their religious ones. So the three of us – Frank, Miriam and I – fall into the pattern we might have adopted had we met at a reception in a Manhattan art gallery, rather than here at a remote, missionary outpost on the upper Orinoco.

We stand around, dancing like Tyrolean yodelers as we slap our knees, calves, shoulders and arms, in a futile effort to drive away the mosquitoes that seem particularly virulent here. Frank, perhaps because of his light colouring, seems even more vulnerable to these pests than we are. Beneath the down on his thick arms, I can see hundreds of bites, that puncture his skin like tiny stigmata.

We talk about the Finger Lakes where Frank hails from in upper New York State, and about the wine for which that region is known. Frank asks me about the Knicks and seems vaguely disappointed when I tell him I'm not a basketball fan. No matter, he says; he'll catch the news later, since the mission has recently installed satellite TV.

Miriam asks him about the Casiquiare, which begins not far from here, but Frank says he has never been along it. Too remote. Not enough people. Not enough souls. I ask him if he ever gets lonely here in Tunatama. He says he doesn't, because of his faith, but he does admit that life is harder than it once was, now that most of his colleagues have left.

"It's become too dangerous," he says. "Because of the FARC."

The Colombian guerillas have recently started to cross the border into Venezuela and kidnap people here – often targeting missionaries because so many of them are known to be American.

"We've already lost two," Frank tells us. "Both of them murdered. We don't want to lose any more."

He shakes his head. FARC is a constant threat, he says. "We've been forced to move our headquarters back from the border. It's just not safe. Not any more."

This is valuable information, which I should absorb. But I don't. Instead, I just let it slide on by.

10

My Personal Wagogo

At El Cejal, we get our first view of an established Yanomami village. I'm intrigued by the prospect, because in the films that we watched before we set out, the Yanomami lived in large circular structures, called *shabonos*, which are unlike anything I've seen. Each *shabono* rested on a skeleton of poles, tied together by vines. It had a single entrance, and a protective roof of leaves that sloped up to the sky. The roof was open at the centre so that smoke from their fires could escape, and inside, all the families in the village lived in their own allotted spaces – sleeping, cooking, playing, fighting and arguing in very open, very public, communal lives.

When we step ashore, the first sound we hear is the piercing blast of a whistle, which I take to be a warning, intended to let the villagers know that a couple of strangers have unexpectedly arrived. The muddy patch of bank where we land funnels away from the river and leads us towards a gap in the undergrowth. There, we follow a narrow track, and after about thirty yards, we see two men approaching. Both are dressed in over-sized tee-shirts that hang loosely over shorts (one of the men) and underpants (the other). There is no sign of a penis-string. I brace myself for a challenge – perhaps even a confrontation – but the two men brush past like busy pedestrians on a London street, not even acknowledging we exist.

A few steps further on, we emerge into a clearing and look slowly around. The village surprises me. There is no *shabono* here. Instead, a number of separate huts with mud walls and palm-thatch roofs stand comfortably spaced about fifty feet apart. It's quiet, with no one in sight. But then another shrill blast from a whistle startles us, and on the other side of the clearing, a man emerges from behind one of the huts, brandishing a machete that he waves in our direction in what I hope is a kind of greeting.

For a brief moment, I think of Stanley entering a Wagogo village in Africa, when he was less than half-way through his 800-mile journey in search of Livingstone. The natives there were armed with machete like knives (and lathered with a foul-smelling clay). They pressed around him, pushing and shoving, and threatening his life. Hopelessly outnumbered – by several hundred to one – Stanley refused to show fear, but instead lashed out with his whip and somehow managed to drive the natives back. "A little manliness and show of power was something the Wagogo needed," he later wrote. "When they pressed on me, barely allowing me to proceed, a few vigorous and rapid slashes right and left with my serviceable thong soon cleared the truck."

Here in El Cejal, I hope I will not be required to show my manliness as the Indian with the machete gives another blast on his whistle. He's a small figure, not much bigger than Y, but he moves with a lot more energy and purpose. For a brief moment, I am somewhat confused, since he does not fit the Yanomami profile I've formed in my head any more than did the two men we passed near the river. No wedge of tobacco extends his lower lip, and nothing repulsive – green or otherwise – hangs from his nose. Instead, he is smartly dressed in an overly-large, Los Angeles Lakers tee-shirt that hangs outside a pressed pair of floppy red shorts.

When he draws near enough to greet us, he speaks in fluent, colloquial Spanish.

"*Hola! Qué tal?*"

"*Muy bien, gracias,*" Miriam tells him.

After a further exchange, we come to understand that the man is the village's soccer coach. He has been blowing his whistle to round up his team – he wants to lead them on a training run – while using the machete to hack back the jungle that's slowly encroaching onto the makeshift pitch. The night before, he tells us, he showed his team a video of *Rocky IV*, which he screened on the village's single, battery-powered television set.

"*Muy bueno,*" he says. "*Muy inspirador.*"

Lucho joins us and takes us around to meet some of the other people he knows in the village. One is a school teacher, who shakes my hand and says I should call him

Davi. He clearly has no inhibitions about using his name – in fact, he insists I write it down in my notebook and peers over my shoulder to make sure I spell it correctly. Three other teachers work in the village, he tells us – and waits while I write this down, too – who are here as part of Chávez's drive to improve the standards of education throughout the country. He stops, and I realise I'm expected to be his Boswell and write *everything* down, so I scribble "improve standards" in my notebook, as he carries on to tell me that the government provides a selection of textbooks, which the children study in the village school. Then, when the children are older, they are sent to a boarding school in the much bigger village of Esmeralda, further up the Orinoco.

I look around with fresh eyes. It all seems so orderly. So civilized. Not at all as I expected. The huts may be mud, but now they seem more like small cottages set around a village green. There's even a dog – albeit skeletal and panting in the heat, but nonetheless trotting along as if it has important business to transact.

The first sign that I might be misreading the situation comes when we arrive at the hut of the headman, or *pata*. Lucho pushes at a wooden board that serves as the door, and we step inside. After several moments waiting for our eyes to adjust to the gloom, I see that I'm standing on a mud floor with a high roof that slopes steeply overhead. In front of me, two wooden poles have been stuck into the floor, with a third one slung horizontally between them. This third pole is draped with loincloths, underpants and shirts, as well as the carcass of an animal I can't identify. A Yanomami man crouches beneath it, holding a machete and apparently guarding a heap of papaya on the mud in front of him.

Next to him, slouched on a white, plastic chair, sits a big-bellied man wearing blue shorts and an angry scowl. This is the headman, Lucho tells me. A huge wad of tobacco is stuffed into his lower lip so that it sticks out like an open bottom drawer; and his teeth, when he shows them, are black with decay. He glares at me with an expression of malice. In the gloom behind him, a hammock swings, and from even further back comes the sound of a baby crying and a woman murmuring in an effort to calm it.

I step forward and present the headman with the

braids of tobacco that we bought in Puerto Ayacucho. The tobacco is still damp, just as it should be, and since the shopkeeper we bought it from assured us that it's of the best quality, I am confident it will be well received. The headman snatches the braids from me and holds them in both hands under his nose as if he's about to gnaw on a bone. Then he hurls them to the ground at my feet. He makes a noise of disgust that needs no translation, and for a long moment, there's a strained silence. I'm not sure how to proceed, but then I remember the Number Ten fish-hooks and pull a small bag of them out of my pack and extend it towards him. He again snatches at the bag, peers inside and examines the fish-hooks, one by one, before he passes them on to the man on the floor with the machete and the heap of papaya.

He grunts then, and dismisses me with a flick of his hand. Lucho smiles. And so, finally, do I.

⤸

With what we assume is the headman's blessing, we

walk around the rest of the village, and find that El Cejal – like a lot of the settlements we've visited along the upper Orinoco – is in a state of transition, with one foot in the past and the other extended towards an uncertain future. At any given moment, we are never quite sure which manifestation we are about to encounter. The Yanomami nomadic way of life has clearly been abandoned, giving way to a settled existence that's heavily dependent on the intermittent contact the river brings with the outside world. Signs of the new can be seen in the plastic chairs, buckets and flip-flops, in the shiny metal tools, and in the modern packaging that doesn't degrade and so remains scattered around as litter; while signs of the old can be seen in the dyed-red loincloths still worn by some of the men and a few of the women.

We see both of these worlds when we wander back to the river and watch a party of hunters as they prepare to leave in a *curiara*, or dugout canoe. One of the hunters wears a Coca-Cola tee-shirt over baggy shorts, and carries a rifle. Another, dressed only in a loincloth, is armed with a bow and a quiver of arrows.

The contrast between them captures the essence of El Cejal in a single image, so I move forward to take a picture. Then I snap one or two more. I'm discreet, staying nearly one hundred yards back, and using a twelve-times zoom. But the man in the loincloth spots what I'm doing and turns towards me.

He pulls an arrow from his quiver and slots it into his bow, then takes deliberate aim. The arrow is pointing directly at me, just as my camera is pointing at him, and through the viewfinder, I can see the tension in his bow as he pulls back the string.

Quickly, I raise both hands and let my camera drop so that it dangles from the strap slung around my neck. I start to back away, both hands in the air, moving a little sideways as the arrow follows me, still aimed at my chest. I don't exactly run, but neither do I dawdle.

Miriam stumbles along beside me. "I think," she says, summoning her best, dinner-party manners, "it might be time to make our excuses and leave."

11

A Race for the Bifurcation

The Casiquiare leaves the Orinoco a few miles east of El Cejal. It has taken a long time for us to get here, but as we approach the source, we suddenly find ourselves in an unexpected race against time. Night is falling, and in the tropics, that happens quickly. Miriam and I stand on the fore deck of the *Iguana* beside the wheelhouse, and strain our eyes in an effort to be first to catch a glimpse of the river. Excitement buoys us, but as we draw near, it is clear that we will not reach the source before dark.

Three minutes later, we are roaring up the Orinoco in the fast boat. Lucho has the tiller, with Leo hunched beside him. A huge wake fans out behind us, and

Miriam's hair streams in the wind. She readies one of our cameras, while I fiddle with a lens on my Minolta. With my head down, I almost miss what I've come so far to see. Lucho hugs the shore, straining for maximum speed against the current. He's chosen to stay close to the Orinoco's northern bank, but the Casiquiare leaves from the southern bank – nearly half a mile away – and from our vantage point, low on the water, its source is almost impossible to see.

Lucho pulls the tiller towards him, and we jet off across the Orinoco. From Humboldt's description, I've been anticipating that something dramatic will mark the spot where the Casiquiare begins its run for the sea. In his *Personal Narrative*, Humboldt gives the impression that the Orinoco – or "Oroonoko", as he spells it – sweeps down from the base of the Delgado Chalbaud mountain where it has *its* source on the Venezuelan-Brazilian border, and is then squeezed by high mountains and a couple of prominent *cerros*, or hills, which force it to shed some of its waters. "The point (where the Casiquiare leaves) the Oroonoko has a very imposing aspect," he writes. "Lofty granitic mountains rise on the northern bank; and amid them are discovered at a distance the Maraguaca and the Duida."

In vain, I scan the jungle for Humboldt's "granitic mountains" and his two prominent hills, the Maraguaca and the Duida. But the land around us is tabletop flat. There is no sign of an imposing aspect; nor any hint that the Oroonoko is being squeezed. Instead, the Casiquiare just slides quietly off to one side, leaving the Orinoco like a slip road from a freeway, and curves away into the jungle.

I make Lucho circle the boat, and in the gathering gloom, Miriam and I fire off dozens of digital shots of the Casiquiare's source, as well as a couple of rolls of 35-mm film. The images we capture show only a sliver of water backed by a strip of jungle, which in turn is topped by a layer of gray, overcast sky. They could have been taken almost anywhere along the upper Orinoco. But that's not the point. There may be nothing distinctive to see, but it's enough for me just to be here, at this unique spot on the Earth's surface. I've seen the sources of many rivers and watched them seep out of the ground in trickles so small I could dam them with just the palm of one hand. But here, the Casiquiare begins its life fully formed – an adult river that's already one hundred yards wide and flowing along at a lively speed.

⌒

A geographer would call the source of the Casiquiare – the point where it leaves the Orinoco – a "bifurcation". That's where one river divides into two, rather than two rivers uniting to become one, which happens at a confluence. To my mind, bifurcations should be rare, since rivers invariably flow downhill, following the steepest slopes that are available to them, and at any given point on the Earth's surface, there should be only one "steepest slope". In reality, bifurcations are relatively common in deltas, for example, or where rivers flow around obstacles and then come together again.

In northern Egypt, for example, the Nile divides near Cairo to create a couple of smaller rivers, the Rosetta and the Damietta, which follow their own routes to the Mediterranean. And in southern Louisiana, near the town of Simmesport, the Mississippi creates an offshoot, the Atchafalaya, which makes its own way to the Gulf of Mexico. These smaller rivers are called "distributaries" – the reverse of tributaries – because they flow out of the main stream rather than into it. But distributaries like these are almost always found close to the sea, where they're effectively part of their parents' deltas; or, if they are just the offshoots of rivers that divide and later come together, they invariably stay safely within their parents' catchment areas.

The Casiquiare is not like this. It does not begin near a delta, and uniquely, it flows not along some alternate route to the sea, but along a course that takes it into an entirely different river system. It's as if a raindrop, falling into the catchment area of the Thames, travels half-way to the sea, but then suddenly has a change of heart and decides to switch course and jump up and over the watershed that separates it from the Severn.

I still don't know how the Casiquiare manages to perform this feat.

We stay in the fast boat and circle the bifurcation until the *Iguana* catches us up. Back on the mother ship, I stand on deck under a pale moon that shimmers through a fragile veil of cloud. It is night, and the waters around us have turned a silken, glossy black that shines like patent leather. As we take our leave of the Orinoco and begin our journey along the Casiquiare, I detect a subtle shift in the sound of the *Iguana*'s engines. They no longer have to work so hard so their pitch has altered – because now, for the first time since leaving Samariapo, we're moving with the current, and not against it.

12

Balancing Risk and Reward

For the next several days, there is little to mark the passing miles. I sit on deck behind my oil drums and watch the jungle roll by in what seems like an endless loop. The settlements we saw on the Orinoco have disappeared, and what limited river traffic there was has now ceased. We've entered a different world, one that consists solely of the river and the jungle – an impenetrable wall of variegated shades of green. Humboldt described the jungle here as "monotonous", but, for me, that's what makes it so impressive. Its impact lies in its scale.

I imagine myself rising from the deck of the *Iguana*

and soaring above the jungle canopy, buoyed up by the clouds of oxygen that are being pumped out by the factory of plants that now surround me. I would look down on an ocean of green that stretches for hundreds, even thousands, of miles in every direction – one billion acres of forest, in which a single acre nourishes and sustains more than 350 tons of flora. It seems an inexhaustible resource, and yet 20 percent of this jungle has already been destroyed. Each day, about 140 species of plant, animal or insect are lost because of deforestation. That's more than 50,000 species every year. I feel privileged to be here, because I know that in another generation or so, most of this jungle will be gone, so future travellers, coming here in a warmer, dryer climate that this area is already experiencing, will see fields and farms as well as an open and parched savannah.

Already, the number – and variety – of fauna has fallen sharply. Many of the early explorers who paddled along rivers like this one saw peccary, tapir, capybara, sloth and black agouti, but all too often their response was to reach for their Winchesters and fire off a couple of rounds, not to get something for the pot, but to test their skills in a kind of "sport".

From the deck, I scan the jungle but see nothing in the way of animal life. From time to time, I glimpse a fresh-water dolphin, or *boto*, as it breaks the surface of the river to breathe; and occasionally my eye is caught by the flash of an Amazon kingfisher in flight, flushed out of the trees by the noise of our engines. But for the most part, I sit in my chair and follow our progress along the river on one of my maps. Meanwhile, I mull over what I've come to think of as the "incident-with-the-arrow" in El Cejal.

I can't seem to let it go. It plays on my mind. It was, of course, entirely my own fault. I knew that the Yanomami do not like to be photographed, since, like many primitive people, they believe that a photograph can capture a part of their souls. Lucho says the incident meant nothing, that the Yanomami hunter would never have shot me, but was just trying to make his point and force me to leave. I think Lucho is probably right, but given the Yanomami reputation for violence, I cannot be entirely sure.

By sheer chance, I have flipped open the book I am reading and found that, on *his* expedition, Stanley, too, encountered "hostile natives". "Arrows were drawn to the head, and pointed at each of us," he writes. "I never saw mad rage or wild fury painted so truly before on human features." I read this, and then I recall that the Yanomami typically dip their arrows in *curare*, a poison that first paralyses and then kills any animal – human or otherwise – it happens to hit. I think about the danger I might have been in, and the risk I might have been flirting with. And then, in a free association, I recall a motorcycle course I recently completed – because it was there that I was accused of never taking *any* risks.

There were ten of us on that course – a mixed bunch of people, including several hikers with visible tattoos and German-army helmets, which they tucked under their arms like top-gun pilots. The course lasted three days, and on the final afternoon, we were required to show off our newly honed skills by riding a route marked out by orange cones. We could take as much time as we wanted, the woman instructor told us. "Just make sure you don't hit any of the cones."

One by one, my fellow students gunned through the route, rolling on their throttles and stomping on their brakes, before roaring off in a series of wheelies that sent many of the cones flying. The woman instructor gave them a thumbs-up of approval. When my turn came, I proceeded at a slow, deliberate pace – and did not hit a single cone. I aced the test, but instead of praise or support, the woman instructor offered me only a withering look.

"Don't you ever take risks?" she said.

But she said it in a way that clearly implied I had missed the point of what riding a motorcycle is all about – and perhaps, too, I had missed the point of what *life* is all about. She made me think: how many times have I shied away from life's opportunities, because I was afraid to assume the risk?

But now, here on the *Iguana* – half way up the Orinoco and along the Casiquiare – I'm forced to contemplate the corollary question: how many times have I put myself in danger, because I was unable to *assess* the risk?

Another day passes. I'm again on deck with my journal. I call it a "journal", because that's how Stanley would have described it, but really it's just a steno notepad. I record the fact that I've had three river-water showers today, none of which did anything to combat the heat, so now sweat again runs down my spine, and the words I write become smeared whenever I accidentally brush my hand across them. I consult my map and estimate that we have now journeyed about one-quarter of the way along the Casiquiare. I make a note of this, too.

Stanley, meanwhile, is more than half-way through *his* journey across Africa, en route to his historic encounter with Livingstone, and at this point, rather than record the number of showers he's had, he takes the time to express his determination: "I will never give up the search," he writes; "no living man can stop me"; and "only death can prevent me". Stanley, of course, faces a lot more danger than a mere "incident-with-the-arrow". For months now, he has laboured under the constant threat of imminent death – from poisonous plants in the jungle; crocodiles in the rivers; lions and leopards on the plains; and leeches and snakes in the swamps. Then, too, he has endured extreme heat and exhaustion; dehydration and starvation (at one point, he goes without food for seven days), *and* he has contracted smallpox, malaria and a bad case of dysentery. All this comes on top of the threat from spear-and-arrow-wielding "natives"; the constant need to repel ambushes; and the pressure of making countless life-or-death decisions. Stanley shrugs everything off – and pushes on regardless.

Of course, in Stanley's day, risk was an integral part of everyday life – and not just for African explorers. Disease, starvation and poverty threatened almost everyone. Today, we've tried to eliminate risk, so at least in Europe we're insured against many of the perils that come with losing a job, falling ill, or failing to stay young. In spite of this – or perhaps because of it – many people court risk artificially, in much the same way they exercise in a gym rather than expend energy during the course of their working days. They canoe the Zambezi, bike the High Atlas, or ride a camel across the Sahara.

Before starting out on this journey, I read a brief news item about a group of adventure travellers who were drowned by a flash flood in a cave in Thailand; and not long before that, I heard of a British teenager on safari in Africa, who was mauled to death by a pride of lions, and of three Americans who were killed in a rock fall while trying to climb Kilimanjaro. I did not know any of these people, but it's a safe bet that all of them thought they were secure and protected. They were lulled into a false sense of security either by what they assumed was the experience of their guides or by the fact that, as high-paying customers, they had the right to expect, at the very least, that they'd be returned home in one, still-alive piece.

When Stanley took risks, he did so with the full knowledge that he might enjoy a commensurate reward – in his case, lasting fame and a considerable fortune. But when adventure travellers take risks, they do so knowing that their only reward is the experience itself and the dubious honour of a "been there, done that" tee-shirt.

As I sit in my chair on the *Iguana*, I wonder about

the chances *I* might be taking. Exactly what is my reward? And what should I risk to attain it?

~

Our days on the Casiquiare have fallen into a somnolent routine. We rise at dawn, then sit, write, read, think, stare at the jungle, sweat and slap at the insects before, in the evening, we again head for our bunks. The main breaks come when we eat meals, which, for the most part, are prepared by Linda. For lunch today, we were served ceviche, vegetables, pasta, papaya, melon, and *arepas* – a Venezuelan specialty that is made from cornmeal, water and salt, which Linda baked into patties and then stuffed with ham and cheese. Linda spends most of her time in the tiny galley, and when not in there, walks the half-a-dozen steps to her bunk and collapses, never reading, seldom talking and rarely sleeping – just gazing into unfocused space. I wonder if she might be clinically depressed.

Natalia plays the hostess, but doesn't seem to relish the role. She speaks to me in English only if I ask her direct questions, so often I feel as if I have gate-crashed what would otherwise be an extended-family gathering. We usually eat with Leo, his mother Justa, and the unidentified researcher with whom I've barely exchanged a word. Lucho also joins us – but only for a bite or two. He's a man of action and finds it hard to sit still. Several times, I have tried to pin him down with questions, but today he said: "Why do you always keep asking? Things are like they are, because that's the way they are" – which I took, at first, to be a distorted form of determinism, but which, more likely, is simple fatalism. I never see the captains, who are confined to the wheelhouse; and Lucho's teenage son makes a shaggy-haired appearance only when everyone else is asleep.

Suddenly there's a commotion, and I quickly look up from my notebook. Justa is leaning over the side of the boat and pointing.

"There!" she shouts. "There!"

I follow her finger and just make out the shape of a monkey. At least, I think it's a monkey – it's too far away for me to be sure – but then it swings, arm over arm, and I can see that, yes, it *is* a monkey, a howler monkey, moving through the top of a *guama* tree. It's the first one we've sighted along the Casiquiare, and even Linda gets off her bunk to take a look. Y, who is in position crouched on the fore deck, doesn't even turn his head.

I settle down again. Luis, the captain's son, comes on deck and pushes a broom around. He's a mischievous kid, about ten years old, and full of the joys of not going to school. His skinny body, dressed in the ubiquitous oversized tee-shirt and footballer's shorts, is often seen flitting around the decks, jumping out at people here, and pinching someone there. Now, he pushes his broom around, shoving it at everyone's ankles so he disturbs them, then he comes and stands at my shoulder to look down at the words I have written in my journal-notepad. I point to a sentence and struggle to translate it into Spanish; but then I realize he can't read English, so it doesn't matter what I tell him. I write a few Spanish words, and he looks at those, then back at me, and grins – and I realize then that he can't read those words either. He darts away, embarrassed that his ignorance has been exposed.

I think about calling him back, but instead I continue to write, scribbling down more of my thoughts.

∽

To my mind, risk can be seen as the product of two distinct factors – the chances that something will happen, and the adverse consequences if that something does indeed happen. So it's possible to write a simple formula:

Risk = Probability of an Event × Adverse Consequences

As a rule, it is easy enough to determine the adverse consequences. In Stanley's case, it was death, while in mine, it is, I hope, more likely to be fear, discomfort, and the need for another river-water shower. But how do you measure the probability? How do you assess the chances of being drowned in a cave, mauled by lions, buried under a rock fall – or shot in the chest by a Yanomami hunter?

The problem here is that most of us get the

probability dangerously wrong. In our minds, we live in a binary world, where things are either black or white, on or off, up or down. We are hard-wired to think in terms of certainty. But certainty is just an extreme form of probability, found at either end of the probability spectrum. You could say that the probability of a certainty is extremely low – yet we see certainty everywhere we look.

After 9/11, Americans were convinced that flying was dangerous, so they stopped getting on planes. But they didn't stop travelling. Instead, they took to their cars, which they were sure were safer. But riding in a car is far more dangerous than flying in a plane – so in the three months after 9/11, the number of Americans killed on the roads notably spiked. If 9/11 killed 3,000 people, then Americans' inability to assess probability – to gauge the relative risks of flying vs. driving – killed at least 1,000 more.

This problem – of measuring probability – mainly arises because people lean too heavily on their intuition. If they flip a coin, for example, they know that the chances of it landing heads-side-up is the same as that of it landing tails-side-up. But if they toss a coin several times and it lands, say, heads-side-up for nine flips in a row, then they will almost certainly bet that the coin will land *tails*-side-up on the next flip – because, of course, it's extremely unlikely that a coin will land the same side up, either heads or tails, as many as ten times in a row.

But their intuition would be wrong – because the knowledge of what the coin has done resides only with them. The coin has no memory. It has no idea what it has been doing. So the next time it is flipped, the probability of it landing heads-side-up – or tails-side-up – remains exactly as it has always been. It is still fifty-fifty.

This is not to say that the chances of a coin landing heads-side-up ten times in a row is also fifty-fifty. To calculate that probability, you need to express each of the fifty-fifty chances as a fraction – that is, as a half – and then, since each event is independent of all the others, multiply – not add – ten of them together:

$$\frac{1}{2} \times \frac{1}{2} \times \frac{1}{2} \times \frac{1}{2} \times \frac{1}{2} \times \frac{1}{2} \times \frac{1}{2} \times \frac{1}{2} \times \frac{1}{2} \times \frac{1}{2} = \frac{1}{1,024}$$

This tells you that if you flip a coin ten times in a row, there are 1,024 possible outcomes. Only one of these outcomes is ten-heads-in-a-row; the other 1,023 outcomes produce other results, so the chances of getting ten-heads-in-a-row are 1,023 to one against – a long way from fifty-fifty.

But now we're into the sphere of mathematics, which most people – even seasoned, coin-flipping gamblers – don't speak, in spite of the fact that it's one of the easiest of the world's languages to learn. If you try to master French, say, then you soon discover that, compared to English, it has a different word for just about everything. There's a lot of vocabulary to learn. It's the same with German, Italian, Dutch – or any of the other 7,000 or so languages that people still speak. But it's not true of mathematics.

In *Through the Looking Glass*, Humpty Dumpty scornfully tells Alice, "When *I* use a word, it means just what I choose it to mean." Mathematicians – like mark-to-model accountants – do that, too, except that they dispense with the words, and just use letters – x and y – and make *them* mean whatever it is they want them to mean. In mathematics, there is no vocabulary, no spelling, no mix of tenses, and not a lot of grammar either, beyond the golden rule that whatever you do to one side of an equation, you must do to the other.

Mathematics is often rejected because no one has employed it to write a poem or a sonnet. But Dirac found anti-matter in one of his equations, and in one of *his*, Einstein discovered the atomic bomb. It's a powerful language, with the ability to describe the smallest particle as well as the Universe as a whole. It also holds the key to gauging probability – and as a result an accurate assessment of the risks that I'm running.

13

Fat and Bloated, Carapaced Corpses

The afternoon passes slowly. The flat, gray sky sits like a lid above us, the air so lifeless I feel as if I'm trapped in a bell jar with only a blurred view of the world outside. There's no one around – not even Y.

I look towards the bow and notice something odd lying on the fore deck. I stand up and walk towards it, climbing down the short, steep ladder that leads to the galley, then scrambling up onto the fore deck. I think I know what it is, but I can't quite believe it. But when I get closer, I can tell that it is what I thought – a small, dry, slender turd lying there on the deck.

Where I live for part of the year in Colorado, I am

used to seeing scat – deer scat, bear scat, even mountain-lion scat – so my mind automatically runs through the various kinds that I'm familiar with. But I'm not in Colorado. I'm here on the Casiquiare – on a boat, surrounded by water – so even if there were deer, bear and mountain lion here, they would not have climbed on board and left behind a tell-tale sign of their presence. Finally, I acknowledge what I already know. It's not animal scat. Instead, it's a small, dried piece of Yanomami feces.

I look around to see if anyone is watching, as if somehow *I* am responsible for the turd being here. There's still no one in sight, so I take the captain's son's broom and use that to prod the feces over the side and into the river.

I later mention this *faux pas* to Miriam. She shrugs, not particularly surprised. But from now on, the fore deck is renamed the nautically incorrect, but nonetheless appropriate, "poop deck".

~ ♦

Every society has rules that govern the main aspects

of life – strict customs and laws that surround landmark occasions like birth, marriage and death, as well as trivial rituals that control the more mundane events that take place during the everyday course of our lives. These rules determine how we behave – in private, usually, as well as in public – and also what we can say. It is these rules that help to differentiate societies. They are the reason we find other cultures absorbing, and for many of us, they are the reason we travel.

As a Brit, I expect people to shake my hand when we are introduced, but not to expand on this greeting by, say, putting a hand on my shoulder, as this would be tantamount to assault. As a Canadian, I expect people to finish each sentence with an upward lilt and the unnecessary, but implied, question that is contained in the exclamation, "eh". And as a newly minted American, I expect people to keep their physical distance, since experience – supported by research – has established that Americans require at least twelve feet of personal space around them to feel comfortable in public; eight feet when they are socializing with people they don't know well; four feet with good friends and acquaintances; and one-and-a-half feet with best buddies, family members, and suitably qualified, health-care professionals.

I do not know what Y expects, but whenever I see him on the *Iguana*, I nod my head because I think it is polite to acknowledge his presence. At the same time, I make no mention of the state of his tee-shirt. Nor do I give any hint that I've noticed his underpants are missing. I simply pretend not to see, in the same way that, at a party, I would studiously ignore a piece of spinach lodged in a gap between another guest's teeth, and not comment if the toupee he was wearing suddenly slipped to one side.

I am sure that in a hundred, small and unknown ways, I am violating Y's unwritten cultural rules, thereby causing him deep and lasting offence. I am not familiar with all of his society's standards, but I do know that along with defecating on a deck, many of the practices that are acceptable to him would not be acceptable to me. For example, among the Yahomami, it is socially – and morally – permissible:

- to rape available women;

- to treat wives as chattels;
- to poke fun at other people's physical defects;
- to abandon malformed babies; and
- to consume the ashes of the dead.

At the same time, it is not permissible:

- to leave unavenged the deliberate killing of one of your clan; and
- to climb into your hammock without wiping your feet.

∽

This morning, Miriam gave Y a tee-shirt. It was a plain tee-shirt with no logos or slogans written across the front. Also, it was clean. Y grabbed it, in the same manner that the headman in El Cejal grabbed for the Number Ten fish-hooks I held out to him. Y did not acknowledge the gift; nor did he acknowledge Miriam. Instead, he just snatched the tee-shirt out of her hand and held it close to his chest.

And why not? If a tree in the jungle yields fruit, you do not stop to say "thank you".

⌒

I try to keep liberal thoughts like this uppermost in my mind, because I do not want to fall into the trap of ethnocentrism and impose my own set of social – or moral – standards on Y. The Yanomami are, after all, a primitive people who scrape out a marginal existence, so they should, perhaps, be excluded from outside evaluation – or, at the very least, be given more rope than might elsewhere be extended to, say, a chief executive who shamelessly manipulates the exercise price of his stock options.

But that approach raises more questions than I am able to answer. Should a "higher" society (like mine) embrace a higher set of moral standards, or is there an absolute set of standards, which all societies should be expected to meet? If the latter, then who sets the standards – and what exactly makes *their* standards absolute? Did God (assuming he exists) write the rules, or were they invented – because if they were invented, then they must be subjective. And that, in turn, must surely mean they should not be judged outside their cultural context.

With thoughts like these, I enter a moral maze, because if I follow my argument through, I am going to conclude that while I do not condone Yanomami actions like rape and the abandonment of malformed babies, I am not in a position to condemn them. This is not a stance I feel comfortable adopting. The only escape from this maze is to affect an anthropologist's role and tell myself that it's enough for me merely to observe. I do not have to make a judgement.

However, I can't help thinking that if I exclude from the moral realm an action like rape or child abandonment, then I reduce its value and say it doesn't matter – either to me or, much more importantly, to the victim. And that can't be right, either.

෴

The next morning, I climb on deck to find that the

rowing boat is gone. So is Leo. And so too is his mother Justa and the nameless researcher. The three of them have been up for most of the night, putting out nets. The researchers' goal – the main reason they've come on this journey – is to assess the size and nature of the fish population in the Casiquiare. No one has done this before, so they aim to establish a base against which future changes can be measured.

Through the early morning mist, I see them in the rowing boat ahead. Not a breath of wind stirs the surface of the river, so their reflections are frozen, as still as statues. As we approach in the *Iguana*, Leo and his mother start to pack up their gear. A pile of netting sits coiled near the stern of their boat, and something live thrashes around in the bottom, just out of sight beneath the gunwales.

When we pull alongside, it's clear that Justa and the researcher are a little despondent. Justa balances near the netting, her hands on her hips, and looks down at their catch – about a dozen-or-so piranha that are now as stiff as clubs. Even to me, it does not look like much of a haul – not after a whole night of fishing. But then

Leo bends down and yanks at one end of whatever it is that's thrashing around. He uses a claw hammer to bludgeon the thing into submission, then with Lucho's help heaves it out of the boat and onto the *Iguana*.

It's a giant catfish – almost five feet long and weighing in at more than thirty pounds. When Leo lifts it up, he grips its tail in both hands and proudly hoists it off the deck. He holds it chest-high, yet its wiry whiskers are still able to brush his feet.

Justa, however, shakes her head. She thinks the catch is much too sparse. A giant catfish and a dozen-or-so piranha cannot be representative of what's in the water. She and the researcher develop a theory. Many of the fish that should inhabit the river have moved off into the jungle to feed in the waters there. The Casiquiare, swollen and bloated from the months of rain, has overflowed its dry-season banks and now swirls beyond the trees and creepers that would normally mark the shore. The fish must have left the main flow of the river to swim among the roots and to eat the fruit that has fallen from the trees, as well as the insects that swarm more prolifically in the jungle.

Leo fetches a large knife from the galley and slits the catfish open from gills to tail, then bends down and buries his hands in the oozing mush that's in its stomach. While Justa makes notes, squinting through glasses that are perched on the tip of her nose, he picks his way through the bloody pulp and tries to establish what the fish has been eating. He relishes the job, and when his hands are red to the wrist, demands that a photograph be taken.

Justa is not so easily pleased. "We'll have to try again," she says. "On another night." She walks away in disgust.

But a little while later, the *Iguana* is filled with a tantalizing aroma of coriander, garlic, turmeric and some other spices that are foreign to me. Linda is in the galley, cooking up a storm. It will be catfish steaks for lunch – and maybe for supper and breakfast, too.

⥲

Another morning passes, and I go down to the lower deck to eat. It sounds so prosaic to say that – as if

I'm on a cruise ship and am just popping along to join the first sitting. Stanley never travelled like this. When he crossed the Makata Swamp, he succumbed to "African fever", which caused a "general lassitude" and a "disposition to drowsiness". That, in turn, lead to a "spinal ache, which, commencing from the loins, ascended the vertebrae and extended around the ribs until it reached the shoulders, where it settled into a weary pain." In a single week, as "small pox and dysentery raged among us," Stanley was "brought to the verge of the grave", losing as much as forty pounds – nearly one-quarter of his body weight – until he was "reduced to a skeleton, a mere frame of bone and skin, weighing 130 pounds."

Yet here I am, *adding* to my weight. The only exercise I get is when I climb up and down the ladder that joins the rear deck and the galley, a journey I make three times a day. I'm already eating too much of Linda's gourmet cooking, and her already sumptuous fare is frequently enhanced by a steady flow of oversized catfish steaks.

For several nights, Justa and the researcher – along

with Leo – have been out in the rowing boat, and each morning they have returned with at least one catfish – far more than we can possibly eat – so the steaks are now stacked up like hamburger patties in the cooler. I now realize that the first one I saw – the fish I thought was so big – was not much more than a tiddler.

"The beeg ones," Leo told me, spreading his arms as wide as they would go, "are this beeg."

I didn't believe him then. But now that I've seen several more specimens pulled out of the river, I can attest to the fact that the "beeg" ones are almost the size of a man – weighing more than one hundred pounds.

~

I feel another twinge of guilt. When Humboldt plied these waters, he did so in an open canoe, and each night he and his companions had to clear a space in the jungle that was large enough to sling their hammocks. With little protection beyond his clothing, he was constantly exposed to attack by mosquitoes, spiders, ants, scorpions, and anything else that could fly, buzz, creep or crawl into his shirt, pants, socks, ears, nose, and other orifices that looked inviting.

It was worse during the day. Then, he complained, the insects swarmed in clouds so dense that they blocked out his noon astronomical observations. "It is impossible," he wrote in his journal, "not to be constantly disturbed by the mosquitoes, *zancudos*, *jejenes* and *tempraneros*, which cover the face and hands, pierce the clothes with their long, needle-formed suckers, and get into the mouth and nostrils, causing coughing and sneezing whenever any attempt is made to speak in the open air."

We fare much better. Because of the distance we intend to cover, we usually travel at night as well as by day, and our constant motion stirs up a breeze that helps keep the insects at bay. Also, we move *with* the current, so, unlike Humboldt, we are out in the main stream, several hundred yards from the sluggish waters that wash through the jungle where the insects really thrive. We are still plagued by hordes of mosquitoes and *jejenes* – tiny, gnat-like insects with a vicious bite that's inversely proportional to their size – and two nights ago, I was woken in my bunk by a cockroach-like insect, the size of a mouse, which crawled under my mosquito net and across my shoulder and down my neck. But we face nothing like the constant harassment that Humboldt was forced to contend with.

But one day, as I climb on deck to watch the dawn break, I find that the *Iguana* is coated with a thick layer of insect corpses – fat, bloated, carapaced corpses that crunch under foot like gravel. Bodies lie everywhere – on their sides, on their fronts, on their backs – with long, hairy feelers and huge, *Alien*-like legs folded in and convulsed in death.

I look around. My oil drums have been moved, and someone – it has to be Leo – has set up a sheet, hung vertically over the clothes line, and beneath it, he has positioned a row of lights, which, during the night would have shone directly onto the sheet. As it is, the *Iguana* is an insect magnet, since, at night, it is the only light-source for hundreds of miles around. But now, with a bank of arc lights shining onto a white sheet, it has been transformed. Every insect in the Orinoco-Amazon basin has been able to spot us; and every one of them seems to have crash-landed – and is now lying prostrate – on our deck.

I am still staring at this scene of devastation when Leo climbs the ladder behind me and scrunches across the deck towards me. He wears a big smile on his face. He's in his element – ankle deep in "eensex". He spreads his arms to embrace them all. They may be dead, his smile seems to say, but – *no se puede tener todo* – you can't have everything.

"Magneeficent," he shouts, raising his face to the sky.

I shake my head and waggle a finger. No, I say. It's not magnificent. It's the twin towers; it's Dresden; it's Hiroshima and Nagasaki rolled into one. I have never seen carnage like this.

He looks disappointed. "You not like?" he says.

"No," I tell him. "I not like."

He seems deflated. After all, this is the main reason *he* has come here – to collect as many insect corpses as he can. Eventually we reach a compromise. Leo agrees to curtail his insect-harvesting and confine it to the next two nights; while I agree to let him show me the insect pinning-boards he keeps under his bunk.

Leo has a lot of pinning-boards, I find – each one filled by regimented rows of insect bodies. Some of the bodies are huge – big enough to be toys. Most have too many legs, as well as bristles that stick out like wire brushes from under their hard, black shells. The flying ones have their wings spread out in fragile fans, while the crawling ones are skewered to the boards by pins through the chest, slightly to the right of the midline.

Leo catches his insects either in his windsock butterfly net (if they are the flying kind) or in what he calls his "killing jar" (if they are the crawling kind). Patience, he says, is always the key – not just to catch them, but also to pin them. If he pins them too quickly, he tells me, there's a better than even chance that some will revive and struggle back to life.

"Even after they are peenned," he says, "and should by then" – he quickly crosses himself – "be dead. Even then, they fight for the life."

14

An Unpredictable
Quantum Leap

More time passes. One evening, Miriam and I lean over the stern rail and idly watch the wake fanning out behind us. Nothing much is happening. The jungle continues to spool around in an unbroken loop, its fifty shades of green turning sombre as the sun quickly sets. Above the throb of the engines, we hear the insects as they prepare for the night – a cacophony of sounds, like an orchestra warming up. Two parrots fly overhead. They are paired for life and fly in formation, a wing span apart. The sky behind them is gun-metal gray with clouds racing in from the north. But then, just for a moment, the clouds part and we see the searing burst of a crimson sunset.

We lean in silence and watch the sun as it paints a bright, Turner sky – a wash of colours that spread above us "like a pot of paint flung in the public's face".

"I think," Miriam tells me, "that you might be getting your Turner muddled up with your Whistler."

The colours slowly fuse – the reds surrendering to yellows, and the yellows to a deep ochre – and we understand, perhaps for the first time, how the tropics can captivate people the way that mountains do, and also the sea. It's an outrageous display of glory, and it holds us transfixed until the colours dim, fading to black as clouds once again blow in from the north.

We stay near the railing, leaning side-by-side in a companionable silence that is occasionally broken by short bursts of conversation that don't go anywhere, because there's no particular place for them to go. They meander around like an aging river, with Turner and Whistler used as stepping stones that lead Miriam to tell me a story about Clifford Styll, the American expressionist who, she says, once sold a painting for a large sum of money, but then found he didn't like the way his patron had hung it.

"So one day, when he was visiting this patron, he used a pen-knife to cut the painting out of its frame, and brought it back to his studio and hung it there."

I nod my head in the darkness.

"Jackson Pollock," I eventually say, "was known to his friends – and some of his enemies, too – as Jack the Dripper."

The conversation moves around, until it returns to the critic John Ruskin, who attacked Whistler for flinging paint pots at the public while simultaneously defending Turner for much the same alleged offence. From there, it progresses to literary critics, and then onto the film critic, Dorothy Parker.

She was a two-fisted drinker, Miriam tells me, who spent much of her time in the Algonquin Hotel in New York, lunching with writers and then drinking them into the ground at night – no mean feat when it was widely acknowledged that the main tool of a writer's trade was a forty-ounce bottle of bourbon or rye.

"Parker once claimed she was so drunk that when

she fell over, she missed the floor." Miriam says. "She also wrote a poem:

"'I wish I could drink like a lady;

"'I'd have one or two at the most.

"'With three I'm under the table;

"'With four I'm under the host.'"

It's the start of a nightly game, "Quotable quotes", we call it. Forgotten sayings by people long-dead. It's something to pass the time as the *Iguana* chugs through the dark.

⤵

It's day six, or maybe day seven. As they merge into one, I'm beginning to lose track of time. As I wait for the next meal, I can't help thinking that when Newton sat under a tree and apocryphally felt an apple bounce off his head, he made an assumption about time that proved significantly wrong.

Newton, of course, was in the process of discovering gravity and writing equations that precisely define it. His equations are still used today – more than three

147

hundred years later – so when a rocket is fired at, say, Saturn or Mars, NASA uses Newton's equations to make the underlying gravitational calculations. And yet those equations are flawed.

Newton made the mistake of assuming that time is a constant, that it is fixed and set – the same for all of us no matter where in the Universe we happen to be or what we might be doing. Newton was smart enough to know he was making this assumption, and said as much in the preamble he wrote to his equations. But as Einstein later showed – in a thought experiment he called a *Gedankenexperiment* – time is far from being a constant. It is, instead, a variable, one that can shrink and expand. It's not universal. It's personal.

> There was a young lady named Bright
> Whose speed was much faster than light.
> She left one day
> In a relative way
> And returned the previous night.

From the wisdom of my plastic chair, I think that

Newton and Einstein might both have been wrong. Here on the *Iguana*, time has certainly slowed. It crawls along at a pace that, in the words of Thomas Hardy, could be comfortably measured "by a one-handed clock". Perhaps it has stopped altogether. Or maybe it has ceased to exist.

Over the years, our views of time have radically changed. The ancient Greeks thought time was circular; so did the Mayans – which makes sense, given the cyclical nature of life. It is a relatively modern, Western idea that time must be linear. And only entropy – with its ever-increasing disorder – says time is so lopsided that it can flow only one way. The three main systems we use to describe the Universe – Newton's equations, Einstein's relativity, and the puzzle of quantum mechanics – are all at odds with this. They say that time is symmetrical, that it works just as well in reverse, moving towards the past rather than just towards the future.

I sit in my chair and peer ahead. I am, symbolically, facing the future – the traditional way in which we in the West view time. But during the Ming dynasty,

Chinese emperors would sometimes take the opposite approach. They felt that since the future is unknown, it can safely be ignored. Only the past is important, because only the past is fixed. So every now and then – both for enlightenment and amusement – an emperor would order his servants to position his throne in a gently flowing river so that it faced downstream, towards the past.

The emperor would then sit on his throne while his servants waded upstream, into the future, and from there they would float small, elaborate boats down the river towards him. The boats were beautifully designed, with multi-coloured sails of paper or silk, and flowers draped across their decks. They were intended to charm and amaze, and when they reached the emperor, he would throw up his hands in delight, thrilled and enchanted by what the future had unexpectedly brought him. The elaborate boats had floated into his present, and now he could watch them for as long as he liked, as they slowly receded into his past.

On the *Iguana*, I turn my chair around so that I'm facing the stern – looking back at the route we've just travelled. But the past I see appears much as I expect the future to be – an unspooling river and jungle. I turn my chair back, aligning it with the arrow of time, so I'm once again looking into the future. I know that my chances of being shot – not by entropy's arrow of time, but by the poisoned arrow of a Yanomami hunter – increase with each day that I spend on the river, because the Second Law of Thermodynamics can be rewritten to say: If anything *can* go wrong, it *will* go wrong – if you give it enough time.

So I have to modify my formula for risk. I need to find room in my equation for time. I cannot overlook it; and nor, like Newton, can I hide it away in a preamble. My formula for risk must therefore become:

$$\text{Risk} = \text{Probability of an Event} \times \text{Time Exposed to that Event} \times \text{Adverse Consequences}$$

I scribble that into my journal-notepad.

⌒

When Humboldt paddled the Casiquiare, he saw a river that he thought was full of potential. Because it joins two of the world's largest river systems, he viewed it as a "natural canal", which one day would be used to ship goods from as far away as Peru to ports like Puerto Cabello that face the Caribbean near Caracas, and then on to the rich markets that, in his day, were just beginning to emerge in North America. The Casiquiare "phenomenon," he wrote, "will one day be so important for all the political connections of nations (that it) unquestionably deserves to be carefully examined."

It has not worked out that way – even though a team of US engineers spent eight fruitless months, in 1942–43, studying the feasibility of using the Casiquiare to transport rubber to the United States, and so avoid U-boat attacks in the South Atlantic; and the Venezuelan and Brazilian governments briefly considered, in 1995, widening and dredging the river so that more of the Amazon could be opened to mining and logging.

Humboldt, however, was a contemporary of Pierre-Simon de Laplace, who believed in determinism. "We may regard the present state of the Universe as the effect of the past and the cause of its future," Laplace wrote, neatly encapsulating the then-prevailing belief that the Universe ran like clockwork and so could be expected to unfold in line with a fixed set of immutable laws. The thinking was, if you understood those laws and collected enough data, then you could accurately foretell the future simply by extrapolating what you knew about the past. This deterministic view created a confidence – bordering on hubris – that many people of Humboldt's era shared. They were convinced that since Nature was ordered, it could also be controlled.

The world that I grew into is a very different place – best characterized by Heisenberg's Uncertainty Principle, which nominally states that you cannot know both the position and the velocity of an electron, but which, more meaningfully, says that underlying what we think we know is a layer of ambiguity and doubt. The world we inhabit is not a focused reality, but is, instead, at a fundamental level a blurred smear of probability. Before Heisenberg, Laplace's certainty had been forced to give ground in many different areas, but the belief persisted that everything was knowable, if only in theory. If something was not known, it was just a matter of time before it was, so you just had to be patient. Heisenberg showed that some things can *never* be known, no matter how much they are studied.

This discovery should not, perhaps, have come as a surprise. The ancient Greeks – just like Humboldt – thought they lived in an ordered, knowable world, but *their* comforting outlook was rudely shattered when Pythagoras developed his eponymous theorem for right-angle triangles, which says that the square on the hypotenuse is equal to the sum of the squares on the other two sides. This theorem would not seem to be much of a threat to anyone's world-view, but when applied to a right-angled, isosceles triangle with two sides equal to one, the hypotenuse becomes the square root of two. And the square root of two is an irrational number – one that, like pi and the Golden Ratio, phi, goes on forever, never repeating and never ending. That upset the Greeks, because it meant that they could draw the hypotenuse, a line of precisely known length – yet never be able to say precisely how long it was.

Heisenberg's principle is often bandied about at the kind of dinner parties where people say, 'it's all relative', and think they are citing Einstein's General Theory of Relativity (which is really about gravity and the curvature of space-time). It has become a cultural cliché, much like the *Mona Lisa* or Munch's *The Scream*. It is often misunderstood, but its real significance lies in the fact that it destroys causality. It breaks the chain that links cause and effect – the comforting chain that we rely on to make the world around us understandable.

We have a need   wired into our brains – to identify a cause for every effect we encounter, so we impose patterns on the events that involve us even when those patterns aren't there. We need a narrative – a story that links cause and effect – to make sense of developments that are, in truth, as unpredictable as they are unknown. In a modern, capitalist world, this is a need we offload onto economists and analysts, who, for a fee, will offer to explain the inexplicable. They have become our new high priests – much-needed imposters and frauds who help us believe that we live in a rational, linear world, when in fact life is a chaotic, random walk. They may offer an explanation of how the past evolved into the present, but they have nothing of value to say about how the present will determine the future.

Right now, on the *Iguana*, I feel as if I am in a world that, although alien to me, is entirely secure. I am confined to a boat, so cannot be threatened by the jungle around me; I am given three (large) meals each day, as well as somewhere (uncomfortable) to sleep each night; and my experience on board leads me to believe that the events of tomorrow will be a repetition of those of today. Rarely has my life seemed so routine. Rarely has my immediate future seemed so settled.

And yet I know I'm at risk – not just because of the inexorable rise of disorder around me, but also because, without causality, even the normally sound rules of mathematics begin to break down, much like the laws of physics at the brink of a black hole. My formula for risk is just an illusion. It doesn't – cannot – apply. *No* formula could, because at a fundamental level, events in our lives are controlled by chance. They're unpredictable – not just unknown, but also unknowable. So it doesn't matter how fluent I am in mathematics, nor how proficient I become in gauging probability, I will still never know the risks I am taking. All I can say for sure is that my life – even if it now seems settled – will at some point take an unpredictable quantum leap in an as-yet-unknown direction.

15

Stickleback Spines and
Tripwire Roots

At last. Lucho gets the fast boat out. He wants to set off on his own, but Miriam and I won't let him; we need to escape from the *Iguana*, if only for a while. By the time we are ready, Leo is roused, and he, too, decides to come along for the ride.

We head downstream, well in advance of the *Iguana*. Like prisoners on parole, we're relieved to break loose from the confines of the deck and our cabin. A kingfisher shoots out of the jungle and flies low over the water, flirting with its own image as it barely skims the surface. Lucho opens the throttle and we give chase, racing along at full speed, the wind in our hair, and, for no discernible reason, all of us laughing. The king-fisher zigs, then zags, and we follow its flight-path until it darts back into the jungle, and Lucho eases up on the throttle. The boat settles into its wake, and we proceed at a more dignified pace.

Lucho steers a course close to the shore and scans the jungle, trying to spot a *manaca* tree. He points to one that pokes high above the canopy – a good head and shoulders above its neighbours – and turns the boat towards it. We slow to a crawl and search for a place to land. It seems impossible. With the river in flood, there are no banks, no shore. In the dry season, perhaps – but not now, not while the Casiquiare seeps into the trees and creepers, and inundates the land.

We edge forward, parallel to the jungle. There's no current – the flow has been stopped by the choking undergrowth, which emits a raw, loamy smell, like a damp basement. Mosquitoes and *jejenes* buzz all around us, and I begin to get a better feel for the misery that Humboldt was forced to endure. Lucho spots a gap in the foliage, and nudges the bow towards it. He guns the motor to give the boat motion, then kills the

159

engine and tips it forward to bring the propeller out of the water. Branches reach down from above and scratch at our faces with angry spikes. We duck our heads, then flatten ourselves below the gunwales as the boat scrapes through the opening. A log lurks low in the water like a caimen, and when we hit it, Leo leaps out and pulls the boat in. He slithers on soft mud, then angles the bow up and drags the boat onto a waterlogged patch of what passes for land.

We step out into the slime and try to keep our balance. We've been in jungles before, but none as dense as this. It's dank and surprisingly cool, like a burrow. Lucho pushes ahead and hacks a hole in the creepers with a sharp, wide-bladed machete. He can't cut a path, but he can make a tunnel. We follow him through, into a dim world of lurking danger. Bent double, we weave our way around screens of lianas and vines, step over roots that cut across our path, and sink ankle-deep into the spongy mud. The mosquitoes land and bite. It's not raining, but it might as well be. Water drips from the canopy above, plopping onto thick leaves armed with stickle-back spines that claw at our eyes.

As we edge forward, the jungle closes in behind us. We make some twists and turns as Lucho cuts a route. We're so focused on the tripwires of roots that snag at our ankles – and the daggers of thorns that stab us from above – that we soon lose all sense of direction. Twenty feet from the river, and we'd be hard-pressed to find it. Lucho presses on, slashing left and right, and manages to navigate his way to the base of the *manaca* tree he saw from the river. He turns to us with a grin.

"So which way back?" he says, knowing we have no idea. To us, the jungle is the same in every direction – a stockade of plants, spiked like barbed wire, which reaches clear to the sky.

Lucho stabs his machete into the ground and draws a knife from his belt, clenching it in his teeth like a pirate. He's brought two strips of cloth, which he ties into rings. He doubles one of the rings and loops it around the base of the tree, then slips his feet into the ring to keep it taut. The other ring he also doubles up, but loops it around the trunk at head-height, holding it tight in his hands. He puts tension on the upper ring and lifts his feet, still in the cloth, then shifts his weight and raises his hands, moving them up the trunk. He repeats this process, raising first his feet, then his hands, and climbs smoothly and quickly until he disappears into the foliage above.

We stare upwards through the dripping creepers and vines, and try to follow his progress. High above, the thick overcast must have parted, because now coins of sunlight dapple the ground. We can't see Lucho, but we can hear him thrashing about. Then comes a muffled shout, and we step back as a branch-full of dark purple berries crashes through the jungle canopy towards us. Another one follows. Then a third. More thrashing around, and Lucho lands in a jump beside us.

We gather up the berries, still on their branches, and follow him back to the boat, each of us trailing a dense aura of mosquitoes and *jejenes*. We toss the berries into the bow and head downstream. The *Iguana* has passed us and is now far ahead. But we are in no hurry to catch it up.

⤿

That evening, we eat catfish steaks washed down with *yucuta de manaca* – a rich, thick drink made from the berries that Lucho collected. Linda has crushed the berries in a slurry of river water and flour to make the *yucata*, which she now serves in a large bucket – an indication, perhaps, of how popular she knows it will be. The drink is nutritious – packed with iron and Vitamin C. It looks potent, but tastes bland. Natalia tells us that in Amazonas, where food can be in short supply, *yucuta de manaca* has become the staple diet. It is also, she says, sold on the Internet as an exotic sports drink – mainly to health-conscious Westerners putting themselves through the rigours of marathon training.

When the meal is over, I ask Justa about the Casiquiare, and how it manages to flow over the watershed that separates the Orinoco from the Amazon basin. As a scientist who seems to know the river, she might be able to offer an explanation.

"It changes direction," she tells me. "Sometimes, the river flows from the Orinoco to the Negro, and sometimes it switches around and flows from the Negro to the Orinoco."

This is a theory I've heard before. It is, in fact, the most commonly held view, based on the idea that since the terrain that surrounds us is as flat as a slate, there's no real watershed for the river to cross. The Casiquiare truly is a "natural canal", just as Humboldt said – a river without a current, which, like time, can reverse course and flow in either direction. This is not a theory that I subscribe to, since I can see for myself that the Casiquiare has a good current, moving along at three, perhaps four, miles per hour. Also, I'm convinced that there must be a watershed somewhere.

Even so, the theory has merit. The basins of the Orinoco and the Amazon *are* remarkably flat. If you stand on the bank of the Amazon near Iquitos, at the foot of the Andes in Peru, you are 1,900 miles from the Atlantic Ocean. Yet you are only 350 *feet* above sea level. It is easy to imagine that a river that joins the two basins might have a flat enough course that allows it to change direction, and in fact several Amazon tributaries do just that – they run downstream into the Amazon during the dry season, then reverse course and flow upstream when the Amazon is in full flood.

Furthermore, the rainy seasons in the Orinoco and Amazon basins occur at different times of the year, so it is possible to picture the surging flood waters of the Orinoco flowing along the Casiquiare with enough force to get up and over a low watershed to reach the Rio Negro; and then, a few months later, find the bloated waters of the Rio Negro flowing in the opposite direction with sufficient strength to spill back over the same watershed and into the Orinoco.

I ask Lucho about Justa's theory. He shakes his head. "No," he says. "It is not correct. The Casiquiare always flows one way. Never two."

〜

The following day, we continue to motor downstream, not much faster than the current. Miriam spends the morning identifying different shades of the jungle's green – moss green, sea green, emerald green, lime green, slime green, olive green, camouflage green, asparagus green, pine green, jade green, sage green, jungle green – while I sit in my chair and make the occasional note in my journal-notepad.

In the afternoon, the captain's son comes on deck and makes a show of swabbing it down. This is normally the job of Lucho's eldest son – the shaggy-haired teenager from a previous marriage – but lately he's been otherwise engaged as he tries to get something going with the babysitter, who is the only likely on-board candidate for his affections. Linda chops at something in the galley, which, no doubt, will turn into dinner. Y is back in position, squatting on the poop deck and staring blankly at the jungle, while Leo stands near the bow and twirls his windsock net in the air.

We're a strange bunch of people. Chance and circumstance have brought us together, but although we are physically close, we remain trapped in our own individual bubbles, cut off by the experiences and life-styles we have left behind but carry with us as mental baggage.

～

That night, I wake up to a strange silence, because for

the first time in a long time, the *Iguana* has stopped.
I wander out of the cabin, and find Lucho with one
of the captains at work by flashlight in the bowels of
the engines. They've dislodged Y from his spot by the
cooler, pulled up a trapdoor outside the galley, and now
stand in the bilges where the engines are mounted on
a stiff metal frame. Their faces are smeared black with
engine grease, exaggerating the whites of their eyes.

"Is there a problem?" I ask.

Lucho shakes his head. He seems upset, even
offended, that I might think there is something wrong
with his boat. The engines, he says, have been running
day and night and now need a service. A quick oil
change, some grease here, maybe there, and we'll soon
be on our way.

He also tells me that we've turned off the Casiquiare, and have moored in a wide lagoon, a mile or so up
a small tributary called the Rio Pacibo.

"No insects," he says, by way of explanation.

I've already heard that there are two kinds of rivers
in the Orinoco-Amazon basins – those that are murky,
like the Casiquiare, their waters full of minerals and

silt; and those that are clear, but stained dark – like English tea – by tannins released from decaying vegetation. The former rivers attract insects, while the latter – being short of oxygen – do not. The Rio Pasiba is one of the latter.

That, at least, is what Lucho claims. But just before dawn, the *Iguana* comes under surprise attack by a swarm of long-tailed wasps. It's our Pearl Harbor. The wasps have the fury of a tropical hail storm. They whiz around us like bullets. I tolerate them at first, but then I find Leo – who should enjoy an invasion like this – hiding in one of the shower stalls. He has locked himself in, and refuses to come out.

"The wasps," he shouts. "I hate them. They are like the singer. They *steeng*."

꒰⁓꒱

The next day, Leo brings one of his pinning-boards to lunch, and places it on the table near Miriam. He knows she doesn't like insects, so he frees one from its pin and nudges it towards her.

He's had a busy morning. For several hours, he stood on the fore deck and waved his windsock net in the air like a conductor with a baton. He has performed like this for several days now, swooping the net in a series of figure eights and catching nothing but air. The net flaps and flutters like a trapped bird as he swishes it around, so it is hardly surprising he's had no luck. But Leo seems happy, looking over his shoulder to make sure that someone is watching.

This morning, however, he suddenly stopped and gave a whoop of delight. He'd finally trapped something. He shouted to his mother and waved at everyone else to gather around. He'd caught a butterfly, about the width of a hand in size, with fragile orange wings and two black circles that mimic startled, panda eyes. It was beautiful — delicate as filigree, yet seemingly strong.

"I will peen it," Leo said. "On one of my boards."

Later that morning I saw him on the fore deck, close to the spot where Y usually crouches. Leo was sprawled out like a sunbather, even though a wide swathe of purple cloud spread over the sky like a bruise. The *jejenes* were out in full force, so Miriam and I were doused in DEET. But Leo refuses to apply insect repellent, so after an hour or so, the exposed parts of his neck and feet had so many bites that his skin looked like a sieve.

"You want picture?" he asked me, when he showed me the rash that his face had become. "For your magazine?"

Now, over lunch, he edges one of his unpinned insects across the table at Miriam. It's not the beautiful butterfly he caught, but a bloated, ugly insect with twisted, scrunched-up legs and two antennae that look powerful enough to detect the echo of the Big Bang. Miriam tries not to recoil. She knows he just wants to gross her out.

"A lot of people eat eensex," Leo says. "Very good. Much protein. You like to taste?"

Miriam politely declines. "Perhaps later," she says.

He feigns disappointment. "Maybe," he says, "I ask Linda to put one in the soup."

16

Lost Land, Fatal Diseases and Dead Fish

Momoni Island sits in the Casiquiare about half-way down from the bifurcation. It's a desolate spot, much as I imagine Devil's Island would be – bleak, soulless, forgotten and unloved except, of course, by the mosquitoes and *jejenes* that swarm over it in thick clouds that spiral up like smoke from a bonfire. It is also home to one of the captains – a man I've seldom seen, since he has spent the entire voyage working and sleeping in the wheelhouse. It is for him that we stop briefly and go ashore, so he can check that his house is still standing. No one is on the island to greet him. In fact, no one is on the island at all. Once, a community lived here, but now everyone has gone except the captain, who stays here alone. Whenever he leaves the island – which seems to be as often as possible – the jungle creeps forward, sneaking up on his house and encircling it with vines that now embrace it but one day will throttle it.

At the end of the 19th century, several thousand people made their homes along the banks of the Casiquiare in small communities like this one. They were a mixed bag of exploited people, who toiled in the jungle tapping the indigenous *árboles de caucho*, or rubber trees. These were the people at the low end of a soaring rubber boom, which began around 1850 – after Charles Goodyear patented the process of vulcanization – and then took off in the 1890s when pneumatic tyres were first produced. By 1908, when the first Model T Fords began to roll off assembly lines in Detroit, the rubber boom looked as if it would go on forever.

In Manaus – the heart of the rubber industry in Brazil – the boom had already brought untold wealth, as growers there exploited a global monopoly. The more successful ones resided in palatial mansions surrounded by the finest imported furniture and furnishings. The men lit their cigars with $100 bills and "watered" their horses from silver buckets filled to the brim with French champagne, while their wives rejected the murky waters of the Rio Negro and shipped their linen to Europe to be laundered there.

As for the city, it indulgently invested in sixteen miles of streetcar tracks, so the rubber barons could glide around in electric trolleys, a first for the Americas. It also built an elaborate telephone system – a first for Brazil – and an electricity grid that could meet the needs of one million people – even though the population numbered, at the time, a mere 40,000. The *pièce de résistance* was the Teatro Amazonas – an Italian Renaissance style opera house, which staged performances by the most prominent entertainers from Europe and America, lured to the jungle by the promise of earning a fortune for a single night's work. Built with the most refined materials – wrought-iron banisters from England, Carrara marble stairs from Italy, and crystal chandeliers from France – the *teatro* stood as a monument to the city's excess.

173

But just as the wealth and extravagance were at their peaks, the rubber boom turned into a bust. The seeds its rapid destruction – both figuratively and literally – were silently reaching maturity on the other side of the world.

～

Back in the 1870s, an arrogant Englishman by the name of Clements Markham worked as head of the Geographical Department of the British India Office in London. Markham – a homosexual with, contemporaries said, a particular fondness for "earthy Sicilian boys" – is best remembered today for the Polar expeditions he helped to mount, and for the cuttings of the *cinchona* tree – a natural source of quinine – that he smuggled out of Peru and shipped to India and other British colonies in the Far East.

Markham would later become President of the Royal Geographical Society (his statue sits outside the Society's buildings on Kensington Gore, while his grim-faced portrait glares down from one of the oak-panelled walls inside), where he would use his connections to try to discredit Stanley since, in Markham's eyes, the man who found Livingstone was too low class (Stanley was illegitimate and had been abandoned to the poorhouse by his mother) and too American to be worthy of anything other than contempt. But back in the 1870s, Markham had other things on his mind than the social standing of Africa's greatest explorer.

As an aggressive imperialist, Markham believed that Britain should reap the rubber-boom benefits rather than an upstart country like Brazil. So in a repeat of his earlier *cinchona*-smuggling, he sent a "Scotch gardener" named Robert Cross to the Amazon with secret instructions to steal as many rubber-tree seeds and seedlings as possible, and bring them to Kew Gardens, on the outskirts of London, where they could be nurtured and grown into mature plants.

At the same time — and perhaps independently — the director of Kew, Dr Joseph Hooker, commissioned another Englishman, Henry Wickham, to perform the same task that Markham had set for Cross. Wickham was a strange choice for Hooker to make since he was not a botanist, he had no proven interest in plants, and he knew little or nothing about how to grow rubber. But Wickham lived at the time in Santarém – an Amazon river-port about half-way between Manaus and the sea – and that gave him a head-start in what, among the world's leading nations, had rapidly developed into an international race to be the first to smuggle rubber-tree plants out of Brazil.

Both Cross and Wickham completed their assignments and brought thousands of seeds and seedlings to London. Most of the seeds failed to germinate, but in the hothouses of Kew, some of the seedlings successfully matured. It is not clear whose seedlings these were – although Wickham claimed both the credit and a knighthood – but in 1876 some of the stronger plants were shipped to Ceylon and Malaya (now Sri Lanka and Malaysia) and cultivated there. By 1910 – as production of the Model T Ford was gearing up – Southeast Asia's neat, plantation rows of mature rubber trees were ready to be tapped.

The South American monopoly was broken. The British gained the wealth they'd expected. And

settlements like Momoni Island quickly – and quietly
– died.

⟿

Today, only two main groups of people live anywhere near the Casiquiare – indigenous tribes like the
Yanomami, and non-native people who still see profit
in the natural resources the area has to offer. The two
groups do not get along. On paper, the indigenous
tribes have the upper hand, since they live within a
protected area called the Upper Orinoco-Casiquiare
Biosphere Reserve. This Reserve – some 30,000 square
miles in area, or about the same size as Scotland – was
set up by the Venezuelan government in 1991, specifically to shelter the native populations by preserving
their habitat and culture. Unfortunately, it does not
do that.

Back in Puerto Ayacucho, we had found out why
when we spoke to a mild-mannered man named Hector
Blanco, who is the Reserve's Coordinator of Environ-
mental Planning. Some 9,000 indigenous people live

in the Reserve, he told us, and for the most part, they are nomadic Indians who still follow a stone-age way of life, deep in the jungle and away from the rivers. They have little or no contact with the outside world, and they would be well-protected were it not for 2,000-or-so illegal miners, or *garimpeiros*, who have invaded their territory. Most of these miners are searching for gold, and they come – in increasing numbers – from Colombia and Brazil. But unlike the ones we saw in Cárida, *these* miners are not individuals panning for nuggets and gold dust, but are organized groups who mine on a near-industrial scale. To get into the country, they pay bribes of about US$8,000, and then spend another US$20,000 to set up their gold-mining operations.

"Individuals don't have access to that kind of money," Blanco told us. "So someone big must be behind them."

The obvious suspect is FARC since it is well known in Venezuela that the illegal miners in the Reserve do not just pay bribes to the National Guard, but they also send money across the border to FARC. Meanwhile, of course, the indigenous people suffer in terms of lost land, poached wildlife, mercury-poisoned fish and exposure to new and deadly diseases. As things now stand, the Yanomami – the largest group of indigenous people in the protected area – experience an infant-mortality rate of between 60 and 70 percent. No one really knows if their overall numbers are rising or falling.

"The research has yet to be done," Blanco told us.

To complicate matters, the funds that Blanco has at his disposal move up and down with the international price of oil – by far the biggest source of Venezuela's government wealth – while the number of miners who come into the Reserve fluctuates with the price of gold. Then, too, the Brazilian government – but not the Colombian one – has cracked down on illegal miners on *its* side of the border, so the number who look for an easier life in Venezuela has steadily risen. The Reserve attempts to attract money from international sources like the UN, but often, it seems, its efforts result only in an increase in the number of government officials who sit behind the wheels of brand new Toyota Land Cruisers in the polluted and grid-locked streets of Caracas.

17

Endangering the Souls of the Dead

Civilization has not encroached on Viriunave – the second Yanomami village we visit. This tiny settlement perches on the eastern bank of the Casiquiare, and because of its isolation, it differs radically from El Cejal.

As we pull into the shore, Y jumps off the *Iguana* and hurries up the slope towards a row of palm-leaf roofs that peek over the top of a muddy bank. It's the first time I've seen him come properly to life. When we follow him into the village, we pass about half-a-dozen, rough-wood huts, then cross an open mud-flat where naked children are fighting over a battered chunk of

Styrofoam, which they take turns to push around in the dirt. The huts appear to be empty, because, as we later discover, all the young men have left the settlement on a two-day hunt, so the only inhabitants still in the village are the headman, the older men, the women and children.

Few visitors stop here, and even fewer boats, so we elicit a kind of interest. But it's a languid one, which the villagers seem too withdrawn – or too lethargic – to express. Perhaps because the young men have all gone, there is little sign of the overt aggression we've been told we might encounter here. The women – about twenty of them altogether – are either pregnant or they carry at least one child slung on a hip in a woven sash. They stand or crouch on the ground, or swing listlessly in hammocks, staring vacantly at us while we try hard not to stare back. They are mostly naked, except for a loincloth, and several of them wear arrow canes stuck in their faces in the traditional, five-point pattern – one through the nose, one in each cheek, and one through the lower lip. The older children stay close to their mothers, their breadstick legs accentuating their swollen bellies, which have been bloated by the parasites that abound in their water and food. They, too, stare blankly at us, nervously twisting their hair or holding tight to their mothers' loincloths.

The older men present squat on their haunches, their lower lips protruding, stuffed full of tobacco. When we approach the headman, we offer him our gifts of Number Ten fish-hooks and the accompanying lead weights. He takes them eagerly, especially the fish-hooks, and passes them on to the women. The red cloth we've brought does not go over so well, but Lucho gives the headman three machetes, which clearly have considerable value. One of the men draws a finger along the edge of a blade, then creases his face in a black-toothed smile as the tension eases.

Without being asked, the headman grants us permission to take a few photographs. This does not sit well with one of the older women, who spits at us and stomps off towards one of the huts. The headman also offers to "paint up a girl", but we tell him, no, we'd rather see his people as they really are. He ignores this, and orders one of the younger girls to decorate her face. A few minutes later, she comes back with wavy, *ontoño*-red lines across her forehead and cheeks, and small, fiery blossoms inserted into her earlobes. Under orders from the headman, she allows herself to be photographed, but clearly she's unhappy. She stares into the middle distance as if by avoiding our gaze, she can somehow make us disappear.

At Lucho's prompting, the headman allows us to wander around. There is no *shabono*, the communal structure that traditionally houses an entire village. Instead, there are just the huts – basic, square, mud-floor constructions, which Lucho calls "*caneyes*". Normally, he tells us, *caneyes* are open-sided, but here by the river, the mosquitoes and *jejenes* are so relentless – even by the standards of the Yanomami – that the villagers have constructed their huts with *majagua*-wood walls. About a dozen of the huts – each one housing three or four families – form an oval around the barren mud-flat where the children were playing.

We peer through one of the doorways and see, in the curve of a hammock, two young girls and a baby. One of the girls wears flowers in her ears and a thin band of beads around her neck. Her entire face is painted a livid red. In front of her on the ground are the remnants of a fire, with a blackened cook-pot, empty and askew, perched on the embers. Further back in the darkness, we can just make out another young girl, her cheekbones and forehead adorned with red, fluted lines; and beyond her, ghostly in the smoke that rises from a hearth, is one of the older women, drying large green leaves of tobacco. When she sees us in the doorway, she immediately becomes agitated, and angrily shoos us away.

⤿

When in the 16th century Europeans began coming to the New World in large numbers, they brought with them a range of diseases, which the indigenous peoples were unable to withstand. To a large extent, the devastation the newcomers wrought was caused by ignorance rather than malignant design. Today, of course, we know better. We know that the Yanomami were able to live in near-total isolation until the 1950s and early 1960s, and we know, too, that they need – and deserve – our considered protection.

Or do we?

In January, 1968, a team of scientists – led by the American geneticist James Neel and accompanied by the anthropologist Napoleon Chagnon – arrived in the upper Orinoco basin to conduct a number of studies on the Yanomami. Their research was funded – surprisingly, perhaps – by the US Atomic Energy Commission, or AEC, a now-defunct civilian agency of the US government.

The AEC had a dubious history. For thirty years – from 1944 to 1974 – it supported more than 430 experiments that exposed around 16,000 people to varying levels of radiation – often without their knowledge or consent. In one experiment, 850 pregnant women were given doses of radioactive iron. In another, hospital patients were injected with small amounts of plutonium. And in a third, retarded children were fed a diet that included radioactive oatmeal. None of these people – all of them American citizens – had any idea of what was being done to them. Nor did they know they were being poisoned by what they might reasonably have assumed was a trustworthy arm of their own government.

Neel had worked with the AEC since it was established in 1947, and belonged to a group that conducted some of the agency's more clandestine tests. However, his scientific work predated even the AEC, as, in 1945, he had helped organize a number of research studies of the few survivors of the nuclear-bomb attacks on Hiroshima and Nagasaki, near the end of the Second World War. His aim then was to study the effects of exposure to a nuclear blast on a human being's ability to regenerate blood.

To the AEC, this made Neel a natural choice to carry out research among the Yanomami, since – in 1968 – the AEC wanted to compare the pathology of atomic-bomb survivors with the pathology of an isolated people who had never been exposed to anything other than natural radiation. This comparison of the two extremes would, the AEC hoped, enable it to establish safety standards for radiation exposure in the United States.

Neel was eager to conduct this research, but he

also wanted to test some of his theories about why certain diseases can wipe out isolated populations like the Yanomami. To this end, he planned to combine his AEC work with a program to inject many of the Indians – perhaps as many as 2,000 – with a vaccine designed to guard against measles. In 1968 – armed with a budget of US$2 million, and with Chagnon functioning as his interpreter – Neel made contact with a number of unsuspecting Yanomami tribes.

As fate would have it, Neel and his team arrived at a time when the Yanomami were suffering from an outbreak of measles – the disease for which his vaccine was tailored, and one against which the Yanomami had no defence. So Neel pushed ahead and aggressively administered his vaccine. There is a big question mark over his decision to proceed in this way, because not only was his research illegal – he did not have the authorization he needed from the Venezuelan government – but also, as Patrick Tierney says in his book, *Darkness in Eldorado*, the vaccine Neel used – called "Edmonston B" – was known to produce extreme reactions in immune-compromised people like the Yanomami.

Three years before, the World Health Organization had advised the medical profession to avoid using Edmonston B, because, it said, "severe reactions are too frequent to permit its wide and general use." No one else – either before or since – has given Edmonston B to an Amazon tribe, and Neel could easily have acquired a more suitable vaccine, given the size of his AEC funding. That would have made the inoculations safer. It would also have made them easier to administer. Edmonston B should not be given on its own, but should instead be injected with a follow-up shot of gamma globulin. On many occasions, Neel did not use the gamma globulin, and this – plus his questionable choice of using Edmonston B in the first place – may have exacerbated the epidemic and significantly raised the number of Yanomami deaths.

Meanwhile, as he went about administering his vaccine, Neel also took samples of Yanomami blood, which he needed to conduct his radiation studies for the AEC. These studies were of no benefit to the Yanomami, so Neel's actions here are considered unethical. First, he was treating the Indians as little more than laboratory animals; and second, he was violating many of the principles laid down by the Nuremberg Code.

This ten-point code derives from the Nuremberg trials of German citizens who had experimented on concentration-camp victims during the Second World War, and its aim is to govern how research on humans is conducted. In Point One, the code explicitly states that in any experiment "the voluntary consent of the human subject is absolutely essential. This means that the person involved ... should have sufficient knowledge ... of the subject matter ... to make an understanding and enlightened decision" about whether or not to participate.

In his best-selling book, *Yanomamö*, Chagnon may have labelled the Yanomami as the "fierce people", but in 1968 it is unlikely that even they could have conceived of an outside world that, a generation before, had been locked for six years in a global conflict, which caused the deaths of some fifty-five million people and culminated in the atomic-bomb killing of more than 300,000 people in just two cities in Japan. Not even their word "*nomohoni*" could have embraced slaughter on *that* scale. So even if Neel had tried to explain the rationale for his radiation experiments, it is unlikely the Yanomami would have understood it. And without their informed consent, the taking of their blood can only be considered as theft.

To the Yanomami today, the loss of their blood is more than just the violation of an ethical code. The Indians believe that when someone dies, all of that person's bodily remains must be destroyed by cremation and the ashes mixed with plantain juice to form a kind of smoothie. The close relatives of the deceased then drink this smoothie so that the dead person's soul remains within the community and is thus able to find peace.

This endocannibalism, as it is called, may seem distasteful to Western sensibilities, but an offshoot of cannibalism, called theophagy, is practised by Catholics every time they take communion. Theophagy is the sacramental consumption of a god, which, of course, is what Catholics do when – symbolically – they eat the body and drink the blood of Christ.

To the Yanomami shamans, the theft of their blood means an essential part of their ancestry has been taken from them. This not only endangers the souls of the dead, but it also has a devastating effect on the living. The Yanomami are convinced that the loss of their blood impedes the ability of their people to survive and that, all by itself, constitutes one of the biggest threats they are now forced to confront.

❧

As we leave Viriunave, I look back at the village from the deck of the *Iguana* and reflect that nearly every outsider-group that has come into contact with the Yanomami has, in one way or another, violated the golden rule of anthropology and somehow managed to do them harm. The missionaries have attacked the Yanomami culture. The illegal miners have damaged their environment. And the experiments of the scientists have threatened their souls.

The next outsider-group to harm the Yanomami will, I am sure, be adventure-travellers. That is, people like us. Already, the headman in Viriunave is beginning to explore the market value of his culture. A few weeks before we arrived in his village, he agreed to stage a traditional dance that was put on – at the wrong time of year – solely for the benefit of a visiting photographer who was working freelance for a major American magazine. The fee was 300,000 bolivares, then worth about US $140.

Miriam and I did not pay for the photographs we took. Perhaps we should have done. But I like to think that since all we did was "come and observe", we did not break that anthropological rule – we did not do any harm. But as I watch Viriunave recede into the distance, I am reminded of a thought experiment, which the physicist, Erwin Schrödinger, dreamt up in the 1930s to highlight the absurdity of quantum mechanics.

In his experiment, a cat is placed inside a box along with a vial of poison. The cat's fate – whether it will live or die – is determined by the random behaviour of a radioactive particle that is also inside the box. If the particle avoids the vial of poison, the cat will live; but if the particle hits the vial and breaks it, the cat will die. Common sense dictates that at any one time, the cat is either dead or alive. But quantum mechanics – which shuns certainty and relies instead on probability – says the cat must be dead *and* alive, both at the same time. Or perhaps it says the cat is neither dead *nor* alive, but is somewhere in between. Either way, the fate of the cat is unknown – even, perhaps, to the cat – until a conscious observer opens the box and peers in.

To my mind, the Yanomami are struggling to exist in a kind of half-way state – hovering, like Schrödinger's cat, between survival and extinction – so perhaps, after all, we, too, have broken the anthropologist's fundamental rule just by being here. Just by observing. Just by opening the box and peering in. Certainly, I think, if we have not done them actual harm, then we have in some way increased their risk. And that is not a comforting thought.

18

Una Problema across the Border

On our last day on the Casiquiare, we pass Culi-
macare Rock, where Humboldt stopped to take
an accurate reading of his position. It's easy to see why.
The rock – the first, significant physical feature we have
seen since leaving Samariapo – looks like Gibraltar's
and juts out of the jungle the way Ayers Rock pokes
out of the Australian desert.

We are now almost exactly two degrees north of the
Equator.

Before long, we begin to sight the first hints of civilization – a hut here, a jetty there – barely visible on the
other side of the river, which has now broadened out so

that it stretches to more than a mile wide. We wave at a passing bongo, and an hour later, a small *curiara* pulls alongside while its occupant – an old man with a face like a gnawed bone – tries to sell us some fish.

Then, finally, under a bright sun that burns off a low, morning mist, we reach our objective the end of the Casiquiare. The jungle has receded to a thin ribbon, which we can just see far in the distance. We are surrounded by water. The Rio Guainia, also in flood, flows in from the north and joins the Casiquiare here at the confluence to form the Rio Negro, which runs southeast to join the Amazon near Manaus.

Once again, I ask Lucho to circle the *Iguana*, while Miriam and I take panoramic shots from the deck to complement the photographs we captured back at the bifurcation. I can understand now how the Casiquiare manages to unite the Orinoco and Amazon river systems – and it's not in the Janus-like way that Justa believes. That common misconception stems from a false interpretation of Humboldt's original text, in which he states that the river "frequently changes its direction". The Prussian explorer did not mean that the

Casiquiare reverses the direction of its flow – merely that it changes direction. In other words, it meanders.

So Lucho is right. The Casiquiare always flows in one direction – from the bifurcation down to the confluence. Of course, at no time does it run uphill. Instead, the bed of the upper Orinoco has been slowly rising – elevated by thick deposits brought down from its source – so it is now a few feet higher than the bed of the Casiquiare. The watershed – the high ground that separates the Orinoco from the Amazon – is therefore right there, *at the bifurcation*. The Orinoco sweeps up to that watershed – the point at which each drop of water must decide whether to stay in the Orinoco and head for the Caribbean, or opt for the Casiquiare and go for the South Atlantic – and simply tips some of its waters over the edge.

Meanwhile, the headwaters of the Casiquiare – and its tributaries – have been eroding back, creeping ever closer towards the Orinoco. For now, the Casiquiare captures between one-quarter and one-third of the water that flows along the upper Orinoco; but that fraction is gradually increasing – it's greater now that it was in Humboldt's day – so at some point, far off in a distant future, the Casiquiare might capture it all. This strange river will then cease to be the geographical oddity it is today. It will no longer link two river systems, but will, instead, be just another tributary feeding into the Rio Negro and the Amazon.

⌐

A celebration is called for. We've travelled from one end of the Casiquiare to the other, just as Humboldt did, so this is as far as the *Iguana* goes. But Lucho still needs to check in with the Venezuelan National Guard in San Carlos – a small river town on the Rio Negro about seven miles downstream from the confluence – to get authorization for the gasoline that will take the *Iguana* back to Samariapo.

He gets the fast boat out, and Miriam and I pile in, followed by Leo. The four of us are in an exuberant mood. We let out a whoop of joy as Lucho guns the engine. We've finally made it, so, yes, a celebration is definitely called for. San Carlos is not much to look at, Lucho warns us, but it does have some stores, a few cafés, and, more importantly, several bars. He opens the throttle as wide as it will go, and we roar down the Rio Negro, the wind ballooning our shirts and blasting the sweat off our faces.

Lucho is right. San Carlos has seen better days. But it still has the advantage of a short airstrip carved out of the jungle, and therefore the prospect of a twin-engined Cessna to take Miriam and me back to Caracas.

We wander around the pot-holed streets while Lucho joins the lines of boat-owners who, like him, must wait for permits to buy their rations of gasoline. Then we slump in the shade, a few yards from the San Carlos dock. It's too hot to do much, but we poke around several of the stores that line the main street. They all stock the same supplies: dusty tins of food; fried pork rinds; dirty bags of salted tortilla chips; boxes of matches; candles; rolls of toilet paper; jars of unwrapped sweets; one or two wrinkled pieces of fruit; and litre-bottles of Coca Cola that are set up in rows like skittles in an alley.

When Lucho joins us, he is disgusted by the long

wait he's had to endure, and by the National Guard and its endless, corrupt bureaucracy. He suggests we cross the river to the other shore. There's another town there, he says. A small place called San Felipe.

"Better food," he tells us. "Better people. We can have lunch at a café I know and celebrate there."

Miriam and I look at each other and shrug. Why not? Leo is against the idea. But if San Felipe is across the river, it's also across the border – in Colombia – and we haven't been to Colombia before. Lunch in San Felipe will give us the chance to tick off one more name on our list of countries we've visited.

And anyway, we think, it *is* only lunch.

⥲

We take the fast boat across the river towards Colombia. The Rio Negro is about three-quarters of a mile wide here, and San Felipe lies only a short distance upstream, so it's a ten- or fifteen-minute ride. Lucho follows the shore on the Colombian side. The banks are high, rising up from the water like levees and blocking our view. He keeps the engine at full speed until we see a dip in the levee that marks the San Felipe dock. Then he throttles back. A makeshift boat ramp angles up from the water's edge, close to a wooden jetty. He aims for that, killing the engine before we arrive so we glide to a stop in a shush of water.

Leo jumps out and ties up the bow. "I no like Colombians," he says.

I ask him why, but he shrugs. "I just no like them."

I put this enmity down to prejudice – a sign of the friction that often exists between two countries that share a border. You can choose your friends – but not your neighbours.

The small dock is empty – no other boats at the jetty, and no other people on the ramp. There are no border controls, either. No customs, and no immigration. That should raise questions, since if there are no officials, then someone else must be in charge.

We walk up the ramp to the top of the levee and come to a sign made of planks of wood that are splitting apart, their paint blistered and dull. "*Bienvenido a San Felipe*" – Welcome to San Felipe. To me, it perfectly captures the louche, languid air of a decaying river port deep in the Amazon jungle, so I take a picture, then a few more.

San Felipe is set slightly back from the river, and the four of us walk towards it, line abreast like the Earps homing in on the OK Corral. The sun is high but shrouded in cloud. Sweat runs down my back in humidity that must be approaching 100 percent.

The town's main street is a dirt strip that's lined by wooden shacks, which seem, from the outside, to sell even less than the stores in San Carlos – mostly machined parts, which are interspersed with tins of food set on end and spaced out like targets in a shooting gallery. But the town does have an edge to it – and, as Lucho says, no Venezuelan National Guard.

We glance into a couple of cantinas with wild-west, bat-wing doors, then a café set with checkered cloths over vacant, white plastic tables. The smooth sound of salsa music shimmies down the street. I take a few more pictures. Because of the heat, only a handful of people are out and about. A couple of men – in jeans and high boots – sit on the boardwalk outside one of the shacks, their chairs tipped back so they have to squint at us from under their wide-brimmed hats. We could be on a film set – in an end-of-the-world, forgotten town, which is waiting for a future that will never arrive.

I take several more pictures, then carry on walking. The café where Lucho wants to eat is located at the far end of town. We cross a square of open ground. It has a mix of huts and shacks on three sides, the fourth side opening out to an expanse of jungle. Lucho stops – he has friends here – and talks to an old man in a sweat-stained hat. I snap a picture of some of the houses set back from the square – they're framed by trees and the jungle that rises behind them – then Lucho leaves his friend, and the two of us walk on to catch up with Miriam and Leo.

And then, suddenly, everything changes. I'm confused at first, but Lucho has stopped again – this time to talk to a younger man, about thirty years old, who looks different from the other men I've seen in town. He's trim, fit and muscled. And he holds himself differently, exuding authority and control. The man wears a black, short-sleeved tee-shirt, which is stretched tight across his chest and tucked into baggy, military-style pants. He has no gun hanging from his hip, but he looks as if he could be a policeman – or maybe a member of the Colombian armed forces.

Leo has stopped, too, and waits beside me.

"*Una problema,*" he says quietly, more to himself than to me.

We listen to what the man is saying to Lucho. The problem has something to do with my camera – I don't know what – but my first thought is that I should not have been taking so many photographs in a border town. But then I think, that's ridiculous. If San Felipe ever had any secrets, they'd have upped and left a long time ago.

Lucho continues to talk to the man, and I hear him say something about Miriam and me being European, not American.

"*No gringos,*" Lucho says. "*No Americanos. Son turistas Ingleses que sólo quieren ver la selva.*" They are tourists from England, who only want to look at the jungle.

Lucho waves his hands to emphasize what he is

saying. But the man isn't listening. He's not looking at Lucho; neither is he looking at me. Instead, he looks at the ground, his hands on his hips, legs apart, in such control that he has no need to engage us.

Then he crooks a finger in my direction. I take a step towards him, and he points at my camera, still not looking up.

"*Dámelo*," he says. Give it to me.

I shake my head, but he reaches out and grabs it – then turns on his heel and marches into the building behind him. I follow him inside, into a dark room that's set up like an office – a metal desk, metal chair, and in one corner a row of metal filing cabinets. The walls are bare. A fan sits in one corner, but it's not switched on.

The man walks straight through the office to a back room and puts my camera in there. He comes out, locks the door behind him, and for the first time looks directly at me. I ask him for my camera, but he shakes his head, and the two of us stare at each other. There's a challenge in his eyes that dares me to confront him. But the moment passes, and he pushes past me into the street.

I follow him outside and hear him tell Lucho that

we should carry on with our plans, we should go on to our café and have lunch, just as we'd intended.

"Come back in twenty minutes," he says. Maybe I will get my camera then.

Lucho protests, but the man holds up his hand and silences him. Lucho nods and moves away. Leo has already gone. When Miriam and I catch the two of them up, I ask Lucho what's going on.

"Is it the camera? Is that the problem? Because I can erase the photos. I don't need them. I don't even want them."

Lucho shakes his head.

"Is he police?" Miriam asks.

"*Yo deseo*," Lucho says. I wish.

It is Leo who tells us. He's walking a little ahead, his head down, shoulders hunched. "Not police," he says. "FARC."

We look at Lucho for confirmation.

"Yes," Lucho says, looking straight ahead. "He's FARC."

19

"They're Terrorists, not Tourists"

Sometimes, events are seen more clearly when viewed obliquely, as if through a prism, rather than when they are seen straight on. I know enough about FARC to appreciate the danger we're in – so I'm worried, there's no doubt about that. But what really alarms me is Leo. Normally so buoyant, so full of life and of himself, he is now pale and withdrawn.

We reach our café and sit at one of the tables. No one else is here, and we're glad about that. We need time to think and decide what to do. Miriam and I huddle with Lucho, while Leo positions himself at a slight angle. His body language says he's not really part of our group; he just happens to be sitting nearby.

No one wants lunch.

I point with my thumb, back the way we have come.

"Are you sure he's FARC?" I ask Lucho.

"I'm sure," he says.

"But how can you be certain?" I'm hoping he might be wrong.

"He's FARC," Lucho says, with finality this time. "He thinks the two of you are American."

"But you told him we aren't. I heard you tell him we're English."

Lucho shrugs. "He doesn't care. To him, the English are as bad as the Americans. He says you are *gringos* either way, because the English are the Americans' *abuelos* — their grandfathers. He says you are all the same."

"But why has he taken my camera?"

Lucho doesn't answer, and I find his silence as worrying as Leo's.

"I think," he finally says, "that I should go and talk to him. Maybe on my own," he adds.

He stands up. Leo stands, too, but only to buy a bottle of coke out of a machine. Miriam and I stay at the table and watch as Lucho heads back into town.

～

It's my conviction that the people who have all the answers in life are the ones who ask the right questions. Sitting at the table, I'm thinking only about my camera. I wonder how I can get it back. My life has taken an unpredictable quantum leap, but I have not been able to go along with it. I remain trapped in my old paradigm, unable to recognize the new reality. I'm focused on my camera, because it's much easier than worrying about FARC.

"They don't want the camera," Miriam says. "They're terrorists, not tourists. They kidnap people and hold them for ransom. Sometimes for years. Then kill them if they don't get paid. They took the camera just to delay us. To keep us waiting here. But it's *us* they want."

"You really think they plan to hold us?" I ask.

Miriam slowly shakes her head. "I don't think they plan to," she says. "I think they already have."

⸏

When Lucho comes back, he does not look happy. He sits down and stares at his hands, clasped on the table in front of him.

"Did you talk to him?" I ask.

Lucho nods.

"And? So what did he say?"

"He wants money," Lucho says. "Ten thousand dollars. For each of you."

Miriam and I look at each other.

"He wants twenty thousand dollars? How the hell are we meant to get *that* kind of money?"

Lucho shrugs. "It's not his problem. He's already called his commander. And he's brought in some of his friends. He tells me I should take my boat – and Leo, too – and leave the two of you here. He says he's going to keep you prisoner until you come up with the twenty thousand dollars."

I sit at the table and try to think. I have two scenarios playing in my head – both possible futures that co-exist, side-by-side, like parallel universes. One involves flying out of San Carlos in a twin-engined Cessna. We could be home in less than twenty-four hours. The other is not so appealing.

It slowly dawns on me that I'm almost as afraid of losing my freedom as I am of losing my life. FARC has held people for years, just as Miriam says. Some have been prisoners for more than a decade – chained like dogs to trees in the jungle. I don't think I can survive that. I don't think I can put my life on hold as year after year goes by, each one as meaningless as another.

"We've got to get out of here," Miriam says.

Well, yes. I've already figured that out.

"No," she says. "I mean we've got to get out of here *now*. Think about it. They want twenty thousand dollars. But even if they get it, they'll only want more. They won't let us go. They'll keep us hostage until they've got everything – and then they'll kill us."

I look across the table at Lucho. He knows FARC much better than I do. I will him to argue, to contradict what Miriam is saying. But he just looks at his hands and then at us, from one to the other and back again.

"We've got to get out," Miriam says, "before they get organized and take us away from here. Venezuela is just across the border, the other side of the river. We'll never get a better chance."

I know she's right. But it's much easier to sit here and pretend that nothing has changed.

Lucho agrees with Miriam. We must leave now, he tells us. We should take his boat and get back to Venezuela. He'll follow later. FARC is no threat to him, but if he's seen with us, then FARC will know he came back to warn us.

Miriam and I stand up. Leo joins us, and the three of us start the long walk back into town. We try not to run, but half-way down the main street, we see the man who took my camera coming out of his office. He's fifty yards away – but he turns and walks away from us, crossing the square of open ground towards the houses that back on to the jungle.

We duck into an alley. The man strides up the steps of one of the houses. There are people there, gathered in a group, some of them armed with rifles slung over their shoulders. The sight of the weapons unnerves me. I know we should continue to walk, just as we'd planned, but the river seems so close.

There is no discussion, no debate. The three of us break into a run, sprinting down the alley, then across a patch of empty ground, past a row of shacks. Our legs are pumping, and I can hear Leo breathing heavily behind me. At any moment, I expect a shout – maybe even a shot. But we keep going, running flat out.

The ground rises up, and we're on top of the levee. There's water below us. We don't stop, but run down to the river, pushing through thick underbrush that slaps at our faces. We're one hundred yards from the boat. A rough trail runs near the river, and we race along that. At the jetty, I briefly wonder if we should wait here for Lucho. But Venezuela is just across the river.

Leo starts the engine, and we pile into the boat. I grab the tiller and point the bow straight out. Half way across, I veer right and head south, cutting a diagonal line towards the opposite bank. We are crouched low in the belly of the boat. Only when we are deep into Venezuelan waters do I risk a glance over my shoulder. There is no one behind. No one in pursuit.

⮑

In San Carlos, we shelter under a tall, leafy tree and pace back and forth. We're close to the river so we can see both ways along it. Not far away, three soldiers in the Venezuelan National Guard lean against a wall, smoking and looking bored. I find myself suddenly glad to see them.

I still feel guilty about leaving Lucho in Colombia, but I tell myself that he's part Indian, part Venezuelan, so FARC *isn't* a threat to him. He's been in San Felipe dozens of times and never come to harm. He has friends there – people who can help and protect him. Lucho would be in danger only if he was seen with us, only if he was seen to be helping us escape. So we *had* to split up and leave him behind.

"Do you think he'll come?" Miriam asks.

"I'm sure he will." It's an expression of hope, more than belief.

"Perhaps we should have waited," Leo says.

⌒

A boat appears on the river, upstream, near the Colombian side. It heads towards us, far in the distance so I'm unable to see who's in it, but there are two people, one in the stern by the tiller, the other low in the bow.

"Is that him?"

It takes several minutes before we can be sure.

"Yes," I say. "It's Lucho."

The boat stops near us. Lucho pays off the man in the stern and steps ashore. His dark skin looks paler than normal, but a big smile creases his face, and we are suddenly grinning, too. We gather around and shake his hand. Leo gives him a hug.

He was able to keep out of sight, Lucho tells us, hiding with some friends. But when he tried to leave, he was spotted by one of the guerillas and taken to the house by the jungle.

"It was like a *película*." Like a film.

There were fourteen guerillas in the house, he says, all of them armed. They thought he had taken his boat and left us behind, still in San Felipe.

"I told them I did try to leave, but my boat was missing. So *you* must have taken it. They didn't believe me at first, but when they saw that the boat was gone, and I was still there and you weren't, they had to accept what I said – they had to accept you'd escaped. They were not pleased," he adds. "But I told them, 'I am just a guide. I have no money.'" He shrugs. "So what could they do?" He pauses for a moment and looks back up the river towards San Felipe. "They also told me, '*despegala pues*'."

I look at Miriam for a translation.

"It means 'fuck off'," she says. "'Fuck off, and don't come back.'"

Lucho grins at her. "I think," he says, "that's what we should do."

20

Pushing the Envelope a Little Too Far

On our flight home, I replay in my mind the events in San Felipe – questioning what I did right, what I did wrong, and what I might have done differently. I did not act like a hero, I know that. But at the same time, I don't think I disgraced myself. Nevertheless, I feel as if I fell short of my expectations. Stanley, I am certain, would have handled himself better.

Once, when *he* was threatened – by a tribe of marauding warriors – he rose to the occasion by joining forces with a band of Arab traders and fought back in a series of extended pitched battles. And when he later faced a mutiny by his servants and porters, he used the strength of his own personality – and a little help from his shotgun – to restore order and impose his will. At no time did he exhibit fear or allow it to divert him from his course. He was never frozen into immobility, but was always up for the next challenge in a way that I could never be.

But as I settle into my aircraft seat, it is not Stanley who is on my mind. Instead, I recall an old Monty Python sketch in which Michael Palin plays a timid accountant who wants to introduce an element of excitement into his life. He decides to retrain and launch himself into a new career – as a lion tamer in a travelling circus. He stops short, however, when he realizes that if he makes the switch, he'll be expected to go *inside* the cage with the lions.

A lot of people use travel to inject excitement into their lives and to see how they measure up when the road ahead develops a few bumps and throws in some unexpected curves. But the fact is, we can no longer duplicate the adventures of Stanley – or even come close to emulating them – so any tests we artificially set will always fall short of the real thing. The Age of the

Explorer has long gone, and has taken with it the kinds of challenges I once thought I wanted to face. I used to lament its passing. But now, I'm no longer so sure. I may still want to paddle the Arctic, climb Mont Blanc, or cycle across the Tibetan plateau. But like Michael Palin's timid accountant, I now realize I do not want to go inside the cage with the lions. I do not want to push the envelope quite that far.

The problem, though – the one I keep coming back to – is how do you know where the boundaries are? How do you come to terms with risk? Bungee-jumping is – quite rightly – considered a dangerous sport. But I don't bungee-jump. I never have and I never will. So for me, bungee-jumping is one of the safest activities I can imagine – right up there with leaping across the Grand Canyon on a rocket-powered bike, another activity I've decided to forego.

In a similar vein, drug companies frequently muddle up risk by trying to spread it over entire populations. They say that you're far more likely to die when bungee-jumping than you are when taking one of their products. But if you don't take the drug in question, then your risk – like mine with bungee-jumping – is reduced to zero. The real risk is assumed by the few people who *do* take the drug, and that risk is frequently unknown, or even unknowable.

I'm confident that my chances of being mauled to death by a lion are extremely small. I also know that I can reduce them to zero if I stay away from lions. But what are my chances if I step into their cage – or even just go on safari?

As I watch the jungle fall away beneath us, I think back to the motorcycle course I took. There, the woman instructor highlighted safety by repeatedly cautioning us to wear thick, heavy clothes – denim or leather – as well as protective, ankle-high boots and gloves. "Dress for an accident," is the way she expressed it, because one day you will surely have one. I thought at the time this was just a piece of sensible advice, but now I see it as zen-like wisdom that might have broad application. It could be a maxim for adventure travel; it could even be one for life.

I'm all too aware that, on the Casiquiare, Miriam and I were in no way "dressed for an accident". We hired a guide we found over the Internet, and did not bother to check him out. We did not know – or particularly care – who else we might be travelling with. We cut ourselves off from any prospect of medical aid, even though we were entering an environment that was alien to us and outside our range of experience. We did not have a Plan B that would help us cope with even one thing going wrong, let alone several at once in what is colloquially known as a "clusterfuck". And perhaps most stupidly of all, we did not tell anyone where we were going when we thoughtlessly crossed the border into an area of Colombia that we knew – or at least should have realized – was under the control of FARC.

But of course, it is always possible to over-dress – to over-analyse whatever it is you plan to do so you never quite manage to screw up the courage that's needed to leave home. The trick, presumably, is to strike a balance – to find a way to come to terms with the disabling uncertainty that otherwise would dominate our lives. With that in mind, I look down at the Rio Negro, as it snakes north towards the Casiquiare, and mentally compose a list of "do's and don't's" that I hope I will follow the next time I feel the urge to travel, or am trying to plan my next step in the somewhat more challenging adventure of life:

- always assess the risks that you face;
- know that this can never be done;
- proceed anyway.

⌇

When we reach home, Miriam and I settle into the celebration that we missed in San Felipe. I open a bottle of champagne and we drink to our health – and to the simple fact that we are indeed home. I may now know that I don't have what it takes to be the intrepid explorer I yearned to be as a child, and it occurs to me briefly that I should be despondent about this. But then I recall that when Stanley finally found Livingstone – after an epic, 800-mile journey that lasted nine months – the two great men toasted each other with a bottle of Sillery champagne that Stanley had carried with him all the way from London. The two men – the greatest explorers of the 19th century, and the 'twin lions' of the Royal Geographical Society – were able to drink only a single bottle between them. But Miriam and I, once we warm to the task, are able to down a bottle of Bollinger each.

Livingstone, the missionary, might not have approved. But Stanley, the explorer and writer, would, I am sure, have been proud.

⸺

The next morning, Miriam presents me with the print-out of a page she has downloaded from the Internet. It is, she says, the last word on risk and how to assess it, and it comes in the form of an ancient Persian proverb, which might be profound – the distillation of centuries of wisdom – or might just be trite.

Either way, it's a proverb that I've started to quote whenever the path ahead is so uncertain, so riddled with unknown pitfalls, that I don't know how – or whether – to advance.

If you have to jump a stream,
and you know how wide it is,
then you will not jump.
But if you do *not* know how wide it is,
then you *will* jump –
and six times out of ten, you will make it.

Afterword

I did wonder, during the brief time that Miriam and I were held captive by FARC, which of my three countries of nationality would try to bail us out – the United Kingdom, Canada or the United States. Probably none of the above. Officially, each of these countries refuses to negotiate with hostage-takers on the grounds that talks would only encourage the terrorist-kidnappers to strike again.

Nevertheless, when we returned home, we felt we should report our brush with FARC to someone. We could have contacted the UK's Foreign and Commonwealth Office, or Canada's Department of Foreign

Affairs and International Trade, but we decided instead to approach the US Department of State – primarily because American citizens are FARC's main foreign targets.

There are two principal reasons for this. First, the United States is still viewed as a bad neighbour in many parts of South (and Central) America, since, at one time or another, it has attacked, invaded, overthrown or exerted undue influence on the governments of many, if not most, of the countries in the region; and second, the United States is in direct conflict with FARC through its eight-year-old Plan Colombia – an on-going program of "aid" by which the US government pays the Colombian military to combat the drug trade and eradicate FARC. This aid – which amounts to more than US$750 million per year – makes Colombia one of the biggest recipients of US largesse outside the Middle East and Afghanistan.

It took a long time for us to get through to the right person at the State Department, but when we did, the official we spoke to showed what we felt was an appropriate level of interest. She took copious notes of what we said, and promised to send word to the US Embassy in Caracas. I am sure she did – and I'm sure, too, that the US embassy took no action at all. There was nothing it could practically do. The State Department's web site already warned that "violence by narco-terrorist groups continues to affect all parts of (Colombia)... and citizens of the US continue to be the victims of threats, kidnappings and other violence." Their message was clear: Don't go there.

Only after we returned home did we fully appreciate the danger we had been in. During the ten years prior to 2006, FARC kidnapped and held hostage literally thousands of people – perhaps as many as 7,500 – including nearly one hundred children. In one year alone – 1998 – it kidnapped 1,016 people, holding them in the most appalling conditions. Many of those people have been held captive for more than ten years, shackled like slaves. Others have simply been shot.

Most of FARC's victims are Colombian nationals – which is why they don't receive the international attention they deserve – but thirty-two have been American citizens. In a daring rescue, carried out in

July 2008, the Colombian army secured the release of the three Americans still being held – Thomas Howes, Keith Stansell and Marc Gonsalves. They had been captured in February 2003, when their plane crashed near Florencia in southern Colombia. Before his release, Thomas Howes spent six months fettered by the neck to another hostage, a 55 year-old Colombian senator named Luis Eladio Pérez; the two men were separated by just fifteen inches of chain.

"We had to walk together," Pérez said, after he was released, "go to the bathroom together, bathe together, eat together. I had to know everything – his snores, his odours. We had to help each other endure. If we had not, we would have killed each other."

The rescue that saved the three Americans also brought freedom to Ingrid Betancourt, a former Colombian presidential candidate with dual (French as well as Colombian) citizenship, who was abducted in 2002. She was FARC's best-known captive. Earlier, FARC had released a Betancourt associate named Clara Rojas – a one-time contender for Colombia's vice-presidency, who was also captured in 2002. In

2004, Rojas gave birth to a child fathered by one of her kidnappers. The child was taken from her. News of the child leaked out when a Colombian police officer emerged from the jungle after he escaped from a FARC encampment. The officer was near death. He had spent eight years in FARC captivity.

When Rojas was released, she brought with her a batch of letters written by other hostages still held in the jungle. They described how they, too, were tied or chained by the neck for periods of years – meanwhile suffering from malaria, diarrhoea, tropical parasites, and a variety of other life-threatening conditions. In one of the letters, a hostage named Luis Mendieta – in his first communication to his family in five years – described the way he had been chained to two other hostages when he was so weak he had to crawl to visit the latrine.

"I had to drag myself through the mud to relieve myself, with only my arms, because I could not stand up," Mendieta wrote. "Then someone ordered chains placed around my neck, tethering me to a stick." He had, he said, "reached the conclusion that kidnapping's suffering knows no limits. But it is not," he added, "the physical pain that wounds us; nor the chains that we wear around our necks that torment us; nor is it the incessant ailments that afflict us. Instead, it's the mental agony, caused by the irrationality of all this. And it's the anger produced by the perversity of the bad, and the indifference of the good."

Mendieta has been a prisoner for more than ten years. There is no indication he will soon be set free.

⁓

As for the Yanomami, they persist with their efforts to recover the blood that was taken from their ancestors. Many other scientists – not just James Neel – gathered samples of blood from the Yanomami in Brazil as well as in Venezuela. Although it is nearly forty years since many of these samples were taken, a number of US laboratories continue to hold them. The Yanomami tribes most directly affected had assumed the samples were destroyed decades ago, but some samples were employed in the Human Genome Diversity Project

– an international effort to find the genetic similarities and differences in the human race.

The US laboratories report that they have stopped using the blood in their research, but they also claim that they cannot return it to the Yanomami, because they are unable to isolate those samples taken from the Yanomami in Venezuela from those taken from the Yanomami in Brazil. Since it is not possible to return the right blood to the right people, the laboratories say, the blood must remain with them.

Meanwhile, the Upper Orinoco-Casiquiare Biosphere Reserve, which was intended to give the Yanomami in Venezuela a degree of protection, continues to falter. The Reserve has never benefited from a fully developed operational plan, so its activities remain mired in internecine disputes, political power plays, and the conflicting interests of the many parties that claim to have jurisdiction over the area.

⤳

As the Reserve withers away from neglect, the number

of adventure travellers continues to grow. Those travellers seeking adventure originate now, not just in the United Kingdom, the United States, and Germany – the three biggest adventure-travel markets – but also from countries that are new to the game, like China, India, Russia and Brazil.

Since April, 2007, adventure travellers who live in the UK have been able to consult a set of standards that can help them evaluate the risks they might face. More importantly, perhaps, the standards also help them assess whether the company or organization they plan to travel with has good safety-management systems in place to deal with those risks.

The standards – endorsed by the Royal Geographical Society, which helped draw them up – have the bureaucratic designation, BS 8848, with the "BS" in this instance standing for British Standards, and the "8848" signifying the pinnacle of adventure-travel achievement – the summit of Mount Everest, which stands at 29,029 feet, or 8,848 metres.

Bureaucratic though they may sound, the standards have a solid, practical value. They are not designed to eliminate risk, nor to take the 'adventure' out of adventure travel. Instead, they're intended to *identify* the risks, and to make sure that adventure travellers know what to do when, inevitably, something goes wrong.

The standards were developed in response to the unnecessary death of a young woman named Claire Eisenegger, who, in 1999, set off on what she thought would be a safe, but exhilarating, adventure-travel trip to Borneo. It was not meant to be a long trip – just a summer expedition before she began her studies for a medical degree at the University of Nottingham.

Claire – a fit eighteen-year-old – travelled with an experienced gap-year company that takes young people to remote corners of the world – partly to give them a challenge, and partly to assist the communities and cultures they encounter along the way. In Claire's case, the social objective was to help construct an orang-utang sanctuary that would not just protect the animals in an environmentally friendly way, but would also give the local people a possible means of financial support.

Claire never made it to Borneo. On the second night of an acclimatization stop-over on a remote island near Singapore, she complained of a headache. Her temperature rose, she began to feel drowsy, and then she started to vomit. After suffering convulsions, she slipped into a coma, and within a matter of hours, Claire was dead – a victim not of a virulent tropical disease, but of something as apparently innocuous as becoming too hot.

Officially, Claire died of heat stroke – but more accurately, she died because neither she, nor anyone around her, understood the risks that she faced, nor how to cope with them. To give meaning to her death – and to help other families avoid unnecessary tragedy – Claire's father, Peter Eisenegger, initiated the process that lead to the writing of the BS 8848 standards. To date, there are no equivalent standards in either the United States or Canada. To my mind there should be, because they would shift the focus to its proper place, and that is on our ability to react to the unexpected, rather than on our failure to predict it.

❧

Finally, the Casiquiare continues to be ignored and forgotten. But for how long remains unclear. South America is the region of the world that is experiencing the fastest growth in "number of visits" by adventure travellers. At the same time, "jungle tourism" ranks high on most adventure-travellers' lists, accounting for some five million visits per year, and the Amazon basin is understandably the jungle tourists' most popular destination. The Casiquiare – that strange river that once enthralled Europe with its apparent ability to flow uphill – may soon be rediscovered, and perhaps subjected to a tsunami of visitors who neither know, nor care, about the mystery that surrounded it for so long.

Authors' notes

* One question we are often asked is: how do two
people write one book, especially a book like this,
which is presented entirely from one point of
view. We felt that although we both experienced
the journey and wrote the manuscript together, it
would be a better book if it was written in the first
person singular rather than in the plural. We did
not want to keep writing "we" said this, or "we"
did that, because it would sound as if we were
joined at the hip or maybe just twinned at the
keyboard – which, fortunately, we are not.

* The map on the endpapers shows – correctly – that if you are travelling up the Orinoco, you will come first to El Cejal, then the bifurcation where the Casiquiare begins, and then to the Christian mission at Tamatama. In the text, we changed this order, because on our journey, we doubled back on ourselves and visited Tamatama first, then El Cejal, and then left the Orinoco by way of the bifurcation.

* The Yanomami – as we call the Indians in this book – are sometimes referred to as the Yanomamo (with or without a diacritical mark over the final "o"); but they are also known as the Yanomama or even, at times, the Yanomamos.

The word "yanomamo" means "human being" in the Yanomami language, and this is the word that the anthropologist, Napoleon Chagnon, used to refer to the Indians. It has since been adopted by those people who support Chagnon and his various theories.

If you use the term "Yanomami", you are sometimes thought to be signalling that you oppose Chagnon, or that you are neutral. We use it partly because we are neutral, but also because "Yanomami" is now the term that is most commonly accepted. We are not sure where the word came from, but one theory holds that it was coined by Italian missionaries – "Yanomami" being the Italian plural of "Yanomamo".

As for "Yanomama", we have no idea how that arose, but "Yanomamos" is the Spanish plural of "Yanomamo".

* On another topic altogether – in the sphere of mathematics – the Yanomami have words for "one" and "two", but any number higher than that is simply referred to as "many". This basic way of counting was developed in our Western, Eurocentric culture about 5,000 years ago, in the time of the Sumerians, and appears to be used by some animals as well as by one or two species of birds.

In his book, *Number, the Language of Science*, Tobias Dantzig tells the story of a farmer who is plagued by a crow that keeps eating his grain. The crow lives in a tower where the farmer stores his grain, and every time the farmer enters the tower – intent on shooting the crow – the bird flies off to the safety of a nearby tree. There it waits until it sees the farmer leave, and then it returns to the tower.

One day, the farmer decides to outwit the crow, and enters the tower with a friend. As usual, the crow flies off to the nearby tree and waits. The friend leaves the tower, but the farmer stays behind, hoping the crow will be fooled into thinking the tower is empty and so once again safe. But the crow stays in the tree, waiting until the farmer also leaves.

The next day, the farmer goes into the tower with two friends. Again the crow flies off to its tree, and when the two friends leave, the crow stays away, still waiting for the farmer to leave.

On the third day, the farmer enters the tower with three friends, and the crow takes refuge in its tree. The three friends leave, one by one, and this time the crow returns to the tower – where it is unceremoniously shot by the farmer. Crows, it appears, can count to three, but after that, they just see "many". This might seem to put them on a par with the Yanomami, but that is not really the case. The Yanomami *can* count, but like the crow, they lack words for all the higher numbers.

* As an example of how probabilities can be misunderstood, the physicist Leonard Mlodinow, in his book, *The Drunkard's Walk*, revisits the trial of O. J. Simpson, the American football star who was accused – and questionably acquitted – of killing his ex-wife, Nicole. During his trial – in which substantial evidence of his guilt was established – O. J. was portrayed as a serial wife-beater, who then graduated to murder. In his defence, O. J.'s lawyers showed that only one in 2,500 battered wives or girlfriends is ultimately killed by her husband or boyfriend – so any abuse of his wife meant little in terms of establishing whether O. J. was guilty of murder. But as Mlodinow shows, this statistic is irrelevant. The key point – which the prosecution failed to point out – is that O. J.'s wife, Nicole, had actually been murdered, and among the sample group of battered women who are later murdered, the chances of their husbands' or boyfriends' guilt are close to nine out of ten – a long way from one in 2,500. A failure to understand the odds can sometimes get you killed – but it can also set you free.

* Finally, we should say that, as stated in Chapter 12, the chances of a coin landing heads-side-up or tails-side-up is always fifty-fifty, no matter how many times it is flipped. This is true for all two-sided, symmetrical objects with the notable exception of a slice of bread, which, in compliance with Murphy's Law, always lands butter-side-down.

Acknowledgements

W e would like to thank *Geographical*, the publication of the Royal Geographical Society in London, for commissioning us to write an article about the Casiquiare. The article was published in the magazine's July 2006 issue.

Before and after travelling to the Casiquiare, we read a number of books related to our journey and our planned book – all of which were useful, but among which we would like to acknowledge the following:

Bierman, John. *Dark Safari*. Alfred A. Knopf, Inc., 1990.

Borofsky, Robert. *Yanomami: The Fierce Controversy and What We Can Learn From It*. University of California Press, 2005.

Chagnon, Napoleon A. *Yanomamo: The Fierce People*. Holt Rinehart and Winston, 1968.

Dugard, Martin. *Into Africa – the Epic Adventures of Stanley and Livingstone*. Doubleday, 2003.

Ferguson, R. Brian. *Yanomami Warfare: A Political History*. School of American Research Press, 1995.

Good, Kenneth, with David Chanoff. *Into the Heart: One Man's Pursuit of Love and Knowledge Among the Yanomama*. Simon and Schuster, 1991.

Hall, Richard. *Stanley: An Adventurer Explored*. Houghton Mifflin Company, 1975.

Jeal, Tim. *Stanley: The Impossible Life of Africa's Greatest Explorer*. Yale University Press, 2007.

Lindley, David. *Uncertainty: Einstein, Heisenberg, Bohr, and the Struggle for the Soul of Science*. Doubleday. 2007.

Lizot, Jacques. *Tales of the Yanomami: Daily Life in the Venezuelan Forest*. Cambridge University Press, 1985.

Mlodinow, Leonard. *The Drunkard's Walk: How Randomness Rules our Lives*. Pantheon Books, 2008.

Noland, David. *Travels Along the Edge*. Vintage Books, 1997.

Pennington, Piers. *The Great Explorers*. Facts on File, Inc., 1979, and Aldus Books Limited, 1979.

Ritchie, Mark Andrew. *Spirit of the Rainforest: A Yanomamo Shaman's Story*. Island Lake Press, 1996.

Tierney, Patrick. *Darkness in El Dorado: How Scientists and Journalists Devastated the Amazon*. W. W. Norton & Company, 2001.

In addition, we would like to credit an article by Mark M. Anderson, which appeared in *The Nation*, April 30, 2007, for the quote about Humboldt that we use in Chapter 5. We would also like to acknowledge *The Meaning of Tingo*, by Adam Jacot de Boinod, Penguin Press, 2005, which is our source for the Easter Island word "*tingo*" that we cite in Chapter 7. As for the word "*sahel*" – also quoted in Chapter 7 – it is taken from an article in the *New York Times* by Edward Wong, June 3, 2007.

Finally, we would like to acknowledge the films and video recordings we viewed about the Yanomami. These were:

Asch, Timothy, and Napoleon Chagnon. *The Feast*. 1970.

Asch, Timothy, and Napoleon Chagnon. *Moonblood: A Yanomamo Creation Myth as told by Dedeheiwa*. 1974.

Asch, Timothy, and Napoleon Chagnon. *The Ax Fight*. 1975.

O'Connor, Geoffrey. *Contact: The Yanomami of Brazil*. Realis Pictures Inc. 1990.

National Geographic Socicty. *Yanomami Homecoming*. 1993.

About the authors

Richard Starks was born in England and raised there and in the United States and Scotland, where he graduated with a B.Sc. Honours and a post-graduate M.Sc. degree. He has since worked as a writer, editor and publisher of newsletters and magazines in the United States, Canada and the United Kingdom. He has also written for television, and has had five other books published.

Miriam Murcutt is a writer, editor and former marketing executive in the travel and publishing industries. Born in England, she graduated with a M.A. degree, then worked as a writer and editor on magazines before switching into marketing. She too has worked on magazines, books and other publications in the United Kingdom, Canada and the United States.

Along the River that Flows Uphill is the second book the two authors have written together. Their first, called *Lost in Tibet*, is a true-life adventure, set against the political and cultural background of pre-Chinese Tibet. It was published in the United States and is now in its third printing. The authors have recently sold an option for the film and television rights.

The two authors have travelled extensively throughout Europe, Central and South America, the Far East and the Himalayas. They have a website at *www.starksmurcutt.com*, where you can find photographs from their journey along the Casiquiare. The authors can also be contacted by email at *starksmurcutt@msn.com*.